July 2005

The greatest accolade for a follower of Christ is his pronouncement: "*Well done, good and faithful servant!*" Noël Piper skillfully recounts the stories of women who have undoubtedly heard or will hear these words. Their lives call out from the pages of history to quicken our spirits, fanning the desire that we—like these sisters of old—may be found faithful.

Mary A. Kassian, author and speaker


Noël Piper brings to life ordinary women of generations past and present whose testimonies have catapulted them into extraordinary influence upon the women of subsequent generations. Noël's timely insights may well prove to be timeless in their impact upon the lives of women today and for many generations to come. Any woman will delight in the way this look into the past brings inspiration and encouragement for tackling the challenges of today.

Dorothy Kelley Patterson
Professor of Theology in Women's Studies
Southwestern Baptist Theological Seminary

Other Crossway books by
Noël Piper

*Treasuring God in Our Traditions*
*Most of All, Jesus Loves You!*

# FAITHFUL WOMEN & THEIR *Extraordinary* GOD

*Noël Piper*

CROSSWAY BOOKS

A PUBLISHING MINISTRY OF
GOOD NEWS PUBLISHERS
WHEATON, ILLINOIS

Cover design: Josh Dennis

First printing 2005

Printed in the United States of America

Chapter 1, "Sarah Edwards," is adapted from "Sarah Edwards: Jonathan's Home and Haven," in *A God Entranced Vision of All Things* (Crossway Books, 2004).

Unless otherwise designated, Scripture is taken from *The Holy Bible, English Standard Version*. Copyright © 2001 by Crossway Bibles, a publishing ministry of Good News Publishers. Used by permission. All rights reserved.

Scripture references marked KJV are taken from the King James Version.

**Library of Congress Cataloging-in-Publication Data**
Piper, Noël, 1947-
   Faithful women and their extraordinary God / Noël Piper.
      p. cm.
   Includes bibliographical references.
   ISBN 1-58134-673-5 (tpb)
   1. Women in Christianity—Biography. I. Title.
BR1713.P57      2005
270.8'092'2—dc22                                          2005006519

| BP | | 15 | 14 | 13 | 12 | 11 | 10 | 09 | 08 | 07 | 06 | 05 |
|----|----|----|----|----|----|----|----|----|----|----|----|----|
| 15 | 14 | 13 | 12 | 11 | 10 | 9 | 8 | 7 | 6 | 5 | 4 | 3 | 2 | 1 |

# CONTENTS

# DEDICATION

*To the women of Bethlehem Baptist Church*

You blessed me in the past by asking for stories.
Now I am blessed
when I see you following in the footsteps of saints like
Sarah, Lilias, Gladys, Esther, and Helen.

*May you be strengthened with all power,*
*according to his glorious might,*
*for all endurance and patience with joy,*
*giving thanks to the Father,*
*who has qualified you to share in the inheritance*
*of the saints in light.*
COLOSSIANS 1:11-12

# THANK YOU . . .

First, to my family. To Johnny for keeping me focused on our true Center; to Talitha for playing and studying on her own while I worked; to Abraham and Molly and to Benjamin and Melissa for all those impromptu visits Talitha made to your homes.

To Heather and Elizabeth Haas and others for your hospitality to Talitha while I was writing.

To Helen Roseveare for allowing me to tell your story and for so graciously correcting my mistakes.

To Alison Goldhor and George Ferris for explaining to me (and re-explaining) the old-style British monetary values. I still don't get it.

To Carol Steinbach for reading and rereading and for your excellent suggestions, most of which I used. And the ones I didn't, I probably should have.

To my writing group—especially Lucille Travis and Lois Swenson—for truly constructive criticism, chapter by chapter.

To friends at Crossway Books. To Lane and Ebeth Dennis, Marvin Padgett, and Geoff Dennis for your encouragement and help; and to Lila Bishop and Annette LaPlaca for your eye for details.

To our prayer support team for praying and for meals and raking and other gifts of love.

To everyone who spurred me on by asking, "How's the book coming?"

And most of all, "always and for everything to God the Father in the name of our Lord Jesus Christ" (Ephesians 5:20).

# CROSSINGS

## *Introduction*

*O*rdinary Women and Their Extraordinary God. That's what I wanted to call this book. But one husband reportedly said, "I could never give my wife a book with that title! She might think *I* think she's just ordinary." That's probably a good thing for a husband to feel, but I find it reassuring to know that God works with the *ordinary*.

With *Ordinary Women*, I had in mind something like what Jim Elliot said: "Missionaries are very human folks just doing what they're asked. Simply a bunch of nobodies trying to exalt Somebody."[1] Not all the women in this book are missionaries, but I think each would have been the first to tell you she was just an ordinary person.

So you might ask, Why would I want to bother reading their stories? There's just one reason: These ordinary women had an extraordinary God who enabled them to do extraordinary things. And he's the same today for us. "Jesus Christ is the same yesterday and today and forever" (Hebrews 13:8).

That's why we discover unexpected crossings between our lives and the lives of these five women who lived and worked in six nations over a span of more than 250 years. Gladys Aylward, Lilias Trotter, and Esther Ahn Kim speak of their weakness and unsuitability for the tasks God has given them. Haven't we felt that? As Sarah Edwards fulfilled her tedious, humdrum responsibilities as wife and mother, she had little idea of the ongoing impact she would make for generations through her husband and children and others who came into her home. Don't we need that encouragement in our mundane days? Helen Roseveare struggled with the desire to do excellent work when her surroundings limited her to just "good enough." Haven't we felt frustrated when we thought our gifts and abilities weren't being used fully? Esther Ahn Kim learned to *live* for God in her prison, not just to sit and wait for "normal" life to resume. Don't we sometimes feel we are treading water until our "real" life and ministry begin?

---

[1] Elisabeth Elliot, *Shadow of the Almighty* (San Francisco: HarperSanFrancisco, 1989), p. 46.

Each of these women, in the midst of her ordinary life, lived through what we might call a defining experience. From our perspective now, we can see their lives beforehand preparing them for that turning point. And everything afterward is shaped and colored by it.

Sarah Edwards experienced the refining power of God when, for a few days, she was physically and spiritually shaken by his Spirit. Lilias Trotter discovered the joy of serving God wholeheartedly after she made the agonizing decision to turn away from a life devoted to the art she loved. Gladys Aylward simply took each next step, minute by minute, following God's leading after she had almost totally expended her strength and health to deliver 100 children to safety. Esther Ahn Kim learned that God is not handcuffed by the cruelty of people and prison after she, like Daniel's three friends, refused to bow to a false god. Helen Roseveare found God's presence and power precisely at the very moments when she needed them during weeks punctuated by rape, terror, uncertainty, and pain.

With one exception, these women didn't know each other. But I can almost picture each one passing the baton of faithfulness from her generation to the next.

In 1758, as Sarah Edwards lay dying in New England, "she expressed her entire resignation to God and her desire that he might be glorified in all things; and that she might be enabled to glorify him to the last."[2]

Not quite 100 years later in England, Lilias Trotter was born into a family of a similar social standing as the Pierreponts, Sarah Edwards's family.

When Lilias died in 1928 in Algeria, Gladys Aylward was in London trying to persuade her brother and friends that someone needed to take the gospel to China. Soon she realized that God was calling *her*.

In 1940, as Gladys was trekking across Chinese mountains with 100 children, Esther Ahn Kim had already been a prisoner for the gospel's sake for a year in Korea.

Esther was released in 1945, the year that Helen Roseveare, a medical student in England, became a Christian.

And Helen Roseveare's life crosses the years of our lives, as she passes the baton of faithfulness to us, this generation.

More than chronology links these women. Only God knows all the

---

[2] Elizabeth Dodds, *Marriage to a Difficult Man: The Uncommon Union of Jonathan and Sarah Edwards* (Laurel, Miss.: Audubon Press, 2003), p. 169.

crossings among their lives. But we do know that Helen Roseveare was touched by Lilias Trotter's writing and by her personal acquaintance with Gladys Aylward.

> Lilias Trotter . . . is someone [I have] loved for many years. I was given a copy of her "Parables of the Cross" and "Parables of the Christ Life" (in one volume) before I went to the mission field in 1952/3, and this was a treasured possession—until the rebel soldiers destroyed all my library of precious books in the 1964 rebellion. I quote one of her lovely parables—the one about the sepals of the buttercup folding right back to release the flower, without the power to close again—in my new book.[3] And Gladys Aylward stayed at our WEC Headquarters in . . . about 1950—before she returned to work with Chinese orphans in Taiwan. I can remember vividly some of the meetings she spoke at at that time![4]

We can see other "crossings"—similarities of circumstances and feeling and faith. Frail health. Inner-city mission work among the socially "unacceptable." Significance of "insignificant" contacts and conversations. Lack of qualification to be accepted by a mission board. Recognition of death as a gateway to God. A spirit of "independence" that is really dependence on God.

May God give us eyes to see the crossings of these women's lives with our lives. And even more, may we see God more clearly in our own lives because of what we see in the lives of Sarah Edwards, Lilias Trotter, Gladys Aylward, Esther Ahn Kim, and Helen Roseveare.

> *Remember your leaders, those who spoke to you the word of God. Consider the outcome of their way of life, and imitate their faith. Jesus Christ is the same yesterday and today and forever.*
> HEBREWS 13:7-8

That's why I read biography. To remember people who've led the way on the path with God, to consider their lives, and to imitate their faith. Because we have the same God, and he is the same yesterday, today, and forever.

---

[3] See footnote 279.
[4] Personal e-mail from Helen Roseveare, February 25, 2005.

*P*ut on then, as God's chosen ones, holy and beloved,
compassion, kindness, humility, meekness, and patience,
bearing with one another and, if one has a complaint
against another, forgiving each other; as the Lord has
forgiven you, so you also must forgive. And above all
these put on love, which binds everything together in
perfect harmony. And let the peace of Christ rule in your
hearts, to which indeed you were called in one body.
And be thankful. Let the word of Christ dwell in you richly,
teaching and admonishing one another in all wisdom,
singing psalms and hymns and spiritual songs,
with thankfulness in your hearts to God. And whatever you do,
in word or deed, do everything in the name of the Lord Jesus,
giving thanks to God the Father through him.

COLOSSIANS 3:12-17

# SARAH EDWARDS
*Faithful in the Mundane*

In the 1700s in the New World, thirteen small British colonies hugged the Atlantic coast—separate colonies, not one country. America was a mostly unknown continent, not a nation. Beyond the colonies to the west, no European had yet discovered or measured how far the wilderness stretched into the unknown.

New England and the other colonies were Britain's fragile fingertip grasp on the edge of the continent. The colonists were British citizens surrounded by territories of other nations. Florida and the Southwest belonged to Spain. The Louisiana Territory belonged to France. The French, in particular, were eager to ally themselves with local Indians against the British.

Therefore, any story set within this tenuous political context should elicit the sight of garrisons on hilltops, the sounds of shots in the distance, the discomfort of soldiers billeting in homes, the shock and terror of news about massacres in nearby settlements. This was the background of daily life, to a greater or lesser degree, throughout the eighteenth century in the English colonies.

## SARAH PIERREPONT

Into this setting, Sarah Pierrepont was born on January 9, 1710. Her entire life would be played out against the backdrop of political uncertainty and imminent war. Her family lived in the parsonage in New Haven, Connecticut, where her father, James, was pastor. He also played a part in the founding of Yale College and was a leading voice in the church in New England.

Sarah's mother was Mary Hooker, whose grandfather Thomas Hooker had been one of the founders of Connecticut and played a key role in writing their colony's *Fundamental Orders*, probably the first written constitution in history.

As a child of one of the most distinguished families in Connecticut, Sarah's education was the best a woman of that era typically received. She was accomplished in the social skills of polite society. People who knew her mentioned her beauty and her way of putting people at ease. Samuel Hopkins, who knew her later, stressed her "peculiar loveliness of expression, the combined result of goodness and intelligence."[1]

## JONATHAN EDWARDS

By contrast, Jonathan Edwards, her future husband, was introverted, shy, and uneasy with small talk. He had entered college at thirteen and graduated valedictorian. He ate sparingly in an age of groaning dining tables, and he was not a drinker. He was tall and gangly and awkwardly different. He was *not* full of social graces. He wrote in his journal: "A virtue which I need in a higher degree is gentleness. If I had more of an air of gentleness, I should be much mended."[2] (In that time, *gentleness* meant "appropriate social grace," as we use the word today in *gentle*man.)

## SARAH AND JONATHAN

In 1723, at age nineteen, Jonathan had already graduated from Yale and had been a pastor in New York for a year. When his time in that church ended, he accepted a job teaching at Yale and returned to New Haven where Sarah Pierrepont lived. It's possible that Jonathan had been aware of her for three or four years, since his student days at Yale. In those student days, when he was about sixteen, he probably would have seen her when he attended New Haven's First Church where her father had been pastor until his death in 1714, and where the family remained as members of the parish.[3]

Now, on his return in 1723, Jonathan was twenty and Sarah was

---

[1] Quoted in Elisabeth D. Dodds, *Marriage to a Difficult Man: The Uncommon Union of Jonathan and Sarah Edwards* (Laurel, Miss.: Audubon Press, 2003), p. 15. In the writing of this short biography of Sarah Edwards, I am indebted especially to Dodds's book. I have known this work so long, it is possible that I sometimes might have incorporated its thought without appropriate footnote references. I realize there are weaknesses in Dodds's presentation (see my Foreword to the 2003 edition of *Marriage to a Difficult Man*). So I do recommend that interested readers also go to George Marsden's *Jonathan Edwards: A Life*, and Iain Murray's *Jonathan Edwards: A New Biography*, for more careful chronology, theological interpretation, and understanding of the man who so shaped Sarah's life and was so affected by Sarah.

[2] Quoted in Dodds, *Marriage to a Difficult Man*, p. 17.

[3] Iain H. Murray, *Jonathan Edwards: A New Biography* (Edinburgh, Scotland: Banner of Truth, 1987), p. 91.

thirteen, in an era when it was not unusual for girls to be married by sixteen.

As his new teaching job started at the beginning of the school term, it seems he may have been somewhat distracted from his usual studiousness. A familiar story finds him daydreaming over his Greek grammar book, which he probably intended to be studying to prepare to teach. Instead, we find now on the front page of that grammar book a record of his real thoughts.

> They say there is a young lady in [New Haven] who is loved of that Great Being, who made and rules the world, and that there are certain seasons in which this Great Being, in some way or other invisible, comes to her and fills her mind with exceeding sweet delight; and that she hardly cares for anything, except to meditate on Him. . . . [Y]ou could not persuade her to do any thing wrong or sinful, if you would give her all the world, lest she should offend this Great Being. She is of a wonderful sweetness, calmness, and universal benevolence of mind; especially after this Great God has manifested himself to her mind. She will sometimes go about from place to place, singing sweetly; and seems to be always full of joy and pleasure. . . . She loves to be alone, walking in the fields and groves, and seems to have some one invisible always conversing with her.[4]

All the biographers mention the contrast between the two of them. But one thing they had in common was a love for music. Sarah perhaps knew how to play the lute. (In the year of their marriage, one of the shopping reminders for Jonathan when he traveled was to pick up lute strings.[5] That may have been for a wedding musician, or it may have been for Sarah herself.) Jonathan pictured music as the most nearly perfect way for people to communicate with each other.

> The best, most beautiful, and most perfect way that we have of expressing a sweet concord of mind to each other, is by music. When I would form in my mind an idea of a society in the highest degree happy, I think of them as expressing their

4 Quoted in ibid., p. 92.
5 George M. Marsden, *Jonathan Edwards: A Life* (New Haven, Conn.: Yale University Press, 2003), p. 110.

love, their joy, and the inward concord and harmony and spiritual beauty of their souls by sweetly singing to each other.[6]

That imagery was just the first thought-step into a leap from human realities to heavenly realities, where he saw sweet human intimacy as only a simple ditty compared to the symphony of harmonies of intimacy with God.

As Sarah grew older, and Jonathan grew somewhat mellower, they began to spend more time together. They enjoyed walking and talking together, and he apparently found in her a mind that matched her beauty. In fact, she introduced him to a book she owned by Peter van Mastricht, a book that later was influential in his thinking.[7] They became engaged in the spring of 1725.

Jonathan was a man whose nature was to bear uncertainties in thought and theology as if they were physical stress. In addition, the years of waiting until Sarah was old enough to marry must have added even greater pressure. Here are some words he used to describe himself, from a couple of weeks of his journal in 1725, a year and a half before they would marry:

| | |
|---|---|
| December 29 | Dull and lifeless |
| January 9 | Decayed |
| January 10 | Recovering[8] |

Perhaps it was his emotions for Sarah that sometimes caused him to fear sinning with his mind. In an effort to remain pure, he resolved, "When I am violently beset with temptation or cannot rid myself of evil thoughts, to do some sum in arithmetic or geometry or some other study, which necessarily *engages all my thoughts* and unavoidably keeps them from wandering."[9]

## BEGINNINGS OF MARRIED LIFE

Jonathan Edwards and Sarah Pierrepont were finally married on July 28, 1727. She was seventeen. He was twenty-four. He wore a new pow-

---

[6] Quoted in ibid., p. 106.
[7] Dodds, *Marriage to a Difficult Man*, p. 21. (Dodds spelled the name as Peter Maastricht.)
[8] Quoted in ibid., p. 19.
[9] Quoted in ibid. (emphasis added).

dered wig and a new set of white clerical bands given him by his sister Mary. Sarah wore a boldly patterned green satin brocade.[10]

We get only glimmers and glimpses into the heart of their love and passion. One time, for instance, Jonathan used the love of a man and a woman as an example of our love toward God. "When we have the idea of another's love to a thing, if it be the love of a man to a woman . . . we have not generally any further idea at all of his love, we only have an idea of his *actions* that are the *effects* of love. . . . We have a faint, vanishing notion of their *affections*."[11]

Jonathan had become the pastor in Northampton, following in the footsteps of his grandfather, Solomon Stoddard. He began there in February 1757, just five months before his wedding in New Haven.

Sarah could not slip unnoticed into Northampton. Based on the customs of the time, one biographer imagines Sarah's arrival in the Northampton church:

> Any beautiful newcomer in a small town was a curio, but when she was also the wife of the new minister, she caused intense interest. The rigid seating charts of churches at that time marked a minister's family as effectively as if a flag flew over the pew. . . . So every eye in town was on Sarah as she swished in wearing her wedding dress.
>
> Custom commanded that a bride on her first Sunday in church wear her wedding dress and turn slowly so everyone could have a good look at it. Brides also had the privilege of choosing the text for the first Sunday after their wedding. There is no record of the text Sarah chose, but her favorite verse was "Who shall separate us from the love of Christ?" (Romans 8:35), and it is possible that she chose to hear that one expounded.
>
> She took her place in the seat that was to symbolize her role—a high bench facing the congregation, where everyone could notice the least flicker of expression. Sarah had been prepared for this exposed position every Sunday of her childhood on the leafy common of New Haven, but it was different

---

[10] Ibid., p. 22.
[11] Ibid.

to be, herself, the Minister's Wife. Other women could yawn or furtively twitch a numbed foot in the cold of a January morning in an unheated building. Never she.[12]

Marsden says, "By fall 1727 [about three months after the wedding] Jonathan had dramatically recovered his spiritual bearings, specifically his ability to find the spiritual intensity he had lost for three years."[13]

What made the difference? Perhaps he was better fitted for a church situation than for the academic setting at Yale where he taught before accepting the pastoral position. It also seems likely that the recovery was closely related to their marriage. For at least three years prior to this, in addition to his rigorous academic pursuits, he had also been restraining himself sexually and yearning for the day when he and Sarah would be one. When their life together began, he was like a new man. He had found his earthly home and haven.

## SARAH AS WIFE

And as Sarah stepped into this role of wife, she freed him to pursue the philosophical, scientific, and theological wrestlings that made him the man we honor. Edwards was a man to whom people reacted. He was different. He was intense. His moral force was a threat to people who settled for routine. After he'd thought through the biblical truth and implications of a theological or church issue, he didn't back down from what he'd discovered.

For instance, he came to realize that only believers should take Communion in the church. The Northampton church was not happy when he went against the easier standards of his grandfather, who had allowed Communion even for unbelievers if they weren't participating in obvious sin.[14] This kind of controversy meant that Sarah, in the background, was also twisted and bumped by the opposition that he faced.

He was a thinker who held ideas in his mind, mulling them over, taking them apart and putting them together with other ideas, and testing

---

[12] Ibid., p. 25.

[13] Marsden, *Jonathan Edwards*, p. 111.

[14] For more on this, see Mark Dever, "How Jonathan Edwards Got Fired, and Why It's Important for Us Today," in *A God Entranced Vision of All Things: The Legacy of Jonathan Edwards*, ed. John Piper and Justin Taylor (Wheaton, Ill.: Crossway Books, 2004), pp. 129-144.

them against other parts of God's truth. Such a man reaches the heights when those separate ideas come together into a larger truth. But he also is the kind of man who can slide into deep pits on the way to a truth.[15]

A man like that is not easy to live with. But Sarah found the ways to make a happy home for him. She made him sure of her steady love, and then she created an environment and routine in which he was free to think. She learned that when he was caught up in a thought, he didn't want to be interrupted for dinner. She learned that his moods were intense. He wrote in his journal: "I have had very affecting views of my own sinfulness and vileness; very frequently to such a degree as to hold me in a kind of loud weeping . . . so that I have often been forced to shut myself up."[16]

The town saw a composed man. Sarah knew what storms there were inside him. She knew the at-home Jonathan.

Samuel Hopkins wrote:

> While she uniformly paid a becoming deference to her husband and treated him with entire respect, she spared no pains in conforming to his inclination and rendering everything in the family agreeable and pleasant; accounting it her greatest glory and there wherein she *could best serve God and her generation* [and ours, we might add], *to be the means in this way of promoting his usefulness and happiness.*[17]

So life in the Edwards house was shaped in large degree by Jonathan's calling. One of his journal entries had said, "I think Christ has recommended rising early in the morning by his rising from the grave very early."[18] So it was Jonathan's habit to wake early. The family's routine through the years was to wake early with him, to hear a chapter from the Bible by candlelight, and to pray for God's blessing on the day ahead.

It was his habit to do physical labor some time each day for exercise—for instance, chopping wood, mending fences, or working in the garden. But Sarah had *most* of the responsibility for overseeing the care of the property.

---

[15] Dodds, *Marriage to a Difficult Man*, p. 57.
[16] Quoted in ibid., p. 31.
[17] Quoted in ibid., pp. 29-30 (emphasis added).
[18] Quoted in ibid., p. 28.

Often he was in his study for thirteen hours a day. This included lots of preparation for Sundays and for Bible teaching. But it also included the times when Sarah came in to visit and talk or when parishioners stopped by for prayer or counsel.

In the evening, the two of them might ride into the woods for exercise and fresh air and to talk. And in the evening they prayed together again.

## SARAH AS MOTHER

Beginning on August 25, 1728, children came into the family—eleven in all—at about two-year intervals: Sarah, Jerusha, Esther, Mary, Lucy, Timothy, Susannah, Eunice, Jonathan, Elizabeth, and Pierpont.[19] This was the beginning of Sarah's next great role, that of mother.

In 1900, A. E. Winship made a study contrasting two families. One had hundreds of descendants who were a drain on society. The other, descendants of Jonathan and Sarah Edwards, were outstanding for their contributions to society. He wrote of the Edwards clan:

Whatever the family has done, it has done ably and nobly. . . . And much of the capacity and talent, intelligence and character of the more than 1400 of the Edwards family is due to Mrs. Edwards.

By 1900 when Winship made his study, this marriage had produced:
- 13 college presidents
- 65 professors
- 100 lawyers and a dean of a law school
- 30 judges
- 66 physicians and a dean of a medical school
- 80 holders of public office, including:
  - 3 US senators
  - mayors of 3 large cities
  - governors of 3 states
  - a vice president of the US
  - a controller of the US Treasury

---

[19] Pierpont's name had a different spelling than Sarah's maiden name, Pierrepont. Standardized spelling hadn't yet become common practice.

Members of the family wrote 135 books. . . . edited 18 journals and periodicals. They entered the ministry in platoons and sent one hundred missionaries overseas, as well as stocking many mission boards with lay trustees.[20]

Winship goes on to list kinds of institutions, industries, and businesses that have been owned or directed by the Edwardses' descendants. "There is scarcely any great American industry that has not had one of this family among its chief promoters." We might well ask with Elisabeth Dodds, "Has any other mother contributed more vitally to the leadership of a nation?"[21]

Six of the Edwards children were born on Sundays. At that time, some ministers wouldn't baptize babies born on Sundays, because they believed babies were born on the day of the week on which they had been conceived, and that wasn't deemed an appropriate Sabbath activity. But all of the Edwards children were baptized regardless of their birthday.

And all of them lived at least into adolescence. That was rare in an era when death was always very close, and at times this drew resentment from other families in the community.

## THE HOUSEHOLD

In our centrally-heated houses, it's difficult to imagine the tasks that were Sarah's to do or delegate: breaking ice to haul water, bringing in firewood and tending the fire, cooking and packing lunches for visiting travelers, making the family's clothing (from sheep-shearing through spinning and weaving to sewing), growing and preserving produce, making brooms, doing laundry, tending babies and nursing illnesses, making candles, feeding poultry, overseeing butchering, teaching the boys whatever they didn't learn at school, and seeing that the girls learned homemaking creativity. And that was only a fraction of Sarah's responsibilities.

Once when Sarah was out of town and Jonathan was in charge, he wrote almost desperately, "We have been without you almost as long as we know how to be."[22]

Much of what we know about the inner workings of the Edwards

---

[20] Dodds, *Marriage to a Difficult Man*, pp. 31-32.
[21] Ibid., p. 32.
[22] Quoted in Marsden, *Jonathan Edwards*, p. 323.

family comes from Samuel Hopkins, who lived with them for a while. He wrote:

> She had an excellent way of governing her children; she knew how to make them regard and obey her cheerfully, without loud angry words, much less heavy blows. . . . If any correction was necessary, she did not administer it in a passion; and when she had occasion to reprove and rebuke she would do it in few words, without warmth [that is, *vehemence*] and noise. . . .
>
> Her system of discipline was begun at a very early age and it was her rule to resist the first, as well as every subsequent exhibition of temper or disobedience in the child . . . wisely reflecting that until a child will obey his parents he can never be brought to obey God.[23]

Their children were eleven different people, proving that Sarah's discipline did not squash their personalities—perhaps because an important aspect of their disciplined life was that, as Samuel Hopkins wrote, "for [her children] she constantly and earnestly prayed and bore them on her heart before God . . . and that even before they were born."[24]

Dodds says:

> Sarah's way with their children did more for Edwards than shield him from hullabaloo while he studied. The family gave him incarnate foundation for his ethic. . . . The last Sunday [Edwards] stood in the Northampton pulpit as pastor of the church he put in this word for his people: "Every family ought to be . . . a little church, consecrated to Christ and wholly influenced and governed by His rules. And family education and order are some of the chief means of grace. If these fail, all other means are like to prove ineffectual."[25]

As vital as Sarah's role was, we mustn't picture her raising the children alone. Jonathan and Sarah's affection for each other and the reg-

---

[23] Quoted in Dodds, *Marriage to a Difficult Man*, pp. 35-36.
[24] Quoted in ibid., p. 37.
[25] Ibid., pp. 44-45.

ular family devotional routine were strong blocks in the children's foundation. And Jonathan played an integral part in their lives. When they were old enough, he would often take one or another along when he traveled. At home, Sarah knew Jonathan would give one hour every day to the children. Hopkins describes his "entering freely into the feelings and concerns of his children and relaxing into cheerful and animate conversation accompanied frequently with sprightly remarks and sallies of wit and humor . . . then he went back to his study for more work before dinner."[26] This was a different man from the one the parish usually saw.

It is possible to piece together a lot about the Edwards household because they were paper savers. Paper was expensive and had to be ordered from Boston. So Jonathan saved old bills, shopping lists, and first drafts of letters to stitch together into small books, using the blank side for sermon writing. Since his sermons were saved, this record of everyday, sometimes almost modern, details was saved as well. For instance, many of the shopping lists included a reminder to buy chocolate.[27]

## SARAH'S WIDER SPHERE OF INFLUENCE

It was understood by travelers in that colonial time that if a town had no inn or if the inn was unsavory, the parson's house was a welcoming overnight place. So from the beginning in Northampton, Sarah exercised her gifts of hospitality. Their home was well known, busy, and praised.

Sarah was not only mother and wife and hostess; she also felt spiritual responsibility for those who entered her house. A long line of young apprentice pastors showed up on their doorstep over the years, hoping to live with them and soak up experience from Jonathan. That's why Samuel Hopkins was living with them and had the occasion to observe their family. He arrived at the Edwards home in December 1741. Here's his account of the welcome he received.

> When I arrived there, Mr. Edwards was not at home, but I was received with great kindness by Mrs. Edwards and the family and had encouragement that I might live there during the win-

---

[26] Quoted in ibid., p. 40.
[27] Ibid., p. 38.

ter. . . . I was very gloomy and was most of the time retired in my chamber. After some days, Mrs. Edwards came . . . and said as I was now become a member of the family for a season, she felt herself interested in my welfare and as she observed that I appeared gloomy and dejected, she hoped I would not think she intruded [by] her desiring to know and asking me what was the occasion of it. . . . I told her . . . I was in a Christless, graceless state . . . upon which we entered into a free conversation and . . . she told me that she had [prayed] respecting me since I had been in the family; that she trusted I should receive light and comfort and doubted not that God intended yet to do great things by me.[28]

Sarah had seven children at the time—ages thirteen down to one and a half—and yet she also took this young man under her wing and encouraged him. He remembered it all his life.

The impact of Sarah Edwards's assurance in God's working did not stop in that personal conversation. Hopkins went on to become a pastor in Newport, Rhode Island, a town dependent on the slave economy. He raised a strong voice against it, even though many were offended. But one young man was impressed. William Ellery Channing had been adrift till then, looking for purpose in his life. He had long talks with Hopkins, went back to Boston, became a pastor who influenced Emerson and Thoreau, and had a large part in the abolitionist movement.[29]

Hopkins obviously admired Sarah Edwards. He wrote that "she made it her rule to speak well of all, so far as she could with truth and justice to herself and others. . . ." This sounds a lot like Jonathan's early flyleaf musings about Sarah—confirmation that he hadn't been blinded by love.

Hopkins commented on the relationship between Jonathan and Sarah:

In the midst of these complicated labors. . . [Edwards] found at home one who was in every sense a help mate for him, one who made their common dwelling the abode of order and

---

[28] Quoted in ibid., p. 50.
[29] This chain of influence is described by Dodds in ibid., pp. 50-51.

neatness, of peace and comfort, of harmony and love, to all its inmates, and of kindness and hospitality to the friend, the visitant, and the stranger.[30]

Another person who observed the Edwards family was George Whitefield, when he visited America during the Great Awakening. He came to Northampton for a weekend in October 1740 and preached four times. Also, on Saturday morning, he spoke to the Edwards children in their home. Whitefield wrote that when he preached on Sunday morning, Jonathan wept during almost the whole service. The Edwards family had a great effect on Whitefield as well:

Felt wonderful satisfaction in being at the house of Mr. Edwards. He is a Son himself, and hath also a Daughter of Abraham for his wife. A sweeter couple I have not yet seen. Their children were dressed not in silks and satins, but plain, as becomes the children of those who, in all things ought to be examples of Christian simplicity. She is a woman adorned with a meek and quiet spirit, talked feelingly and solidly of the Things of God, and seemed to be such a help meet for her husband, that she caused me to renew those prayers, which, for many months, I have put up to God, that he would be pleased to send me a daughter of Abraham to be my wife.[31]

The next year Whitefield married a widow whom John Wesley described as a "woman of candour and humanity."[32]

## SARAH'S SPIRITUAL CRISIS

Jonathan Edwards was a key player in the Great Awakening, the revival that was sweeping the colonies. He was called on frequently to travel and preach. During this time, the family at home was in the midst of tension over finances. In 1741, Jonathan asked the church for a set salary due to the growing needs of his large family. This caused the parish to scrutinize the lifestyle of the Edwards family, alert for signs

---

[30] Ibid., p. 64.
[31] Ola Winslow, *Jonathan Edwards: 1703-1758: A Biography* (New York: Macmillan, 1940), p. 188.
[32] Dodds, *Marriage to a Difficult Man*, pp. 74-75.

of extravagance. A salary committee of the church ruled that Sarah had to keep an itemized statement of every expenditure.

During this period of public revival and personal stress, in January 1742, Sarah underwent a crisis that she later described to Jonathan. As she recounted her experiences, Jonathan transcribed them. He published her account in *Some Thoughts Concerning the Present Revival of Religion*.[33] For privacy's sake, he didn't reveal her name or gender.

The soul dwelt on high, was lost in God, and seemed almost to leave the body. The mind dwelt in a pure delight that fed and satisfied it; enjoying pleasure without the least sting, or any interruption. . . .

[There were] extraordinary views of divine things, and religious affections, being frequently attended with very great effects on the body. Nature often sinking under the weight of divine discoveries, and the strength of the body was taken away. The person was deprived of all ability to stand or speak. Sometimes the hands were clinched, and the flesh cold, but the senses remaining. Animal nature was often in a great emotion and agitation, and the soul so overcome with admiration, and a kind of omnipotent joy, as to cause the person, unavoidably to leap with all the might, with joy and mighty exultation. . . .[34]

The thoughts of the perfect humility with which the saints in heaven worship God, and fall down before his throne, have often overcome the body, and set it into a great agitation.[35]

We mustn't imagine that she was shut away alone during this two-week period or that every minute was marked by such transport. Jonathan was away from home all except the first two days. So she was responsible for the home—caring for the seven children and the guests and attending special gatherings at church. Probably no one grasped at the time how completely God was shaking and shaping her when she was alone with him. This was only a month after Samuel Hopkins had moved into their home, so his impressions of the family were being formed in the midst of Sarah's most life-changing days.

---

[33] The section that tells Sarah's story is published as Appendix E in ibid. (2003 edition), pp. 209-216.
[34] Jonathan Edwards, *Some Thoughts Concerning the Present Revival in New England*, in *The Works of Jonathan Edwards*, ed. Edward Hickman, 2 vols. (1834; reprint, Edinburgh: Banner of Truth, 1974), p. 376.
[35] Ibid., p. 377.

The effort to explain this period in Sarah Edwards's life is approached very differently by different biographers, leaving us with the challenge of trying to understand what really happened.

Ola Winslow, a biographer who rejected Edwards's theology, used the account of Sarah's experience to minimize the impact of Jonathan's acceptance of outward, active manifestations of the Holy Spirit. Winslow wrote, "The fact that his wife was given to these more extreme manifestations no doubt inclined him to a more hospitable attitude toward them. . . ."[36] The implication seems to be that under normal circumstances Jonathan would have spoken out against such unusual displays as Sarah's, but since he had to account for her experience, he was forced to be more accepting.

Another Edwards expert, Perry Miller, who rejected the idea of anything supernatural, could only conclude that Sarah's story provided Jonathan with a proof case to use against those who thought "enthusiasm" was from Satan. Miller assumes that, although we modern people know such manifestations couldn't really be supernatural, Edwards was old-fashioned and mistakenly thought something supernatural was going on. So, Miller might say, it was convenient for Edwards to have an experience at hand to use as proof against doubters.[37]

Elisabeth Dodds describes Sarah as "limply needful, grotesque— jabbering, hallucinating, idiotically fainting."[38] She calls it a breaking point, and attributes it to Sarah's previous stoicism, her coping with her difficult husband and many children, the financial stresses, Jonathan's criticism of her handling of a certain person, and her jealousy over the success of a visiting pastor while Jonathan was preaching away from home. Dodds says we can't know if it was a religious transport or a nervous breakdown.[39]

Was Sarah's experience primarily psychological? Probably not. It is rare that a person, for no apparent reason, suddenly snaps out of psychological breakdown and is just fine after that. So Dodds, who believes this was indeed some sort of breakdown, suggests that

---

[36] Winslow, *Jonathan Edwards*, p. 205.
[37] Miller's attitude colors his recounting of this event: Perry Miller, *Jonathan Edwards* (New York: W. Sloane Associates, 1949), pp. 203-206.
[38] Dodds, *Marriage to a Difficult Man*, 81. Dodds describes Sarah's experience in chapter 8.
[39] Ibid., p. 90.

Jonathan was acting as an unwitting forerunner of a psychotherapist when he had Sarah sit down and tell him everything that happened.[40] Did her experience have a spiritual cause? It seems likely. We know that no one ever has *totally* pure motives or actions or causes in his or her spiritual activities, but there is no doubt that both Jonathan and Sarah recognized her experiences as being *from* God and *for* her spiritual delight and benefit. Sarah speaks unambiguously of the experience as a spiritual encounter. So a reader needs to ask: Have the Edwardses proved themselves to be people whose judgment in spiritual matters can be trusted? If so, it would be a mistake to try to explain away her understanding of her own experiences. Nor would we want to minimize Jonathan's confirmation of the spiritual nature of Sarah's experience, implicit in his willingness to make the account public.

Stresses over finances, distress at having upset her husband, jealousy over another's ministry—all those things were real in Sarah's life. And God used those things to reveal himself to Sarah, to show her how much she needed him, to uncover her own weakness. And then, when the almost-physical sensations of God's presence came upon her, he was all the more precious and sweet to her, because of what he had forgiven and overcome for her.

We do well to remember Jonathan's early description of her, written in his Greek book. Granted, he was a besotted lover. But he didn't make up his description out of nothing. He was writing about a certain kind of person, and we can see the shape of her, even if it is through Jonathan's rose-colored glasses.

> . . . there are certain seasons in which this Great Being, in some way or other invisible, comes to her and fills her mind with exceeding sweet delight; and that she hardly cares for anything, except to meditate on Him.[41]

That is very close to how she described this adult experience. And remember that as a thirteen-year-old, she loved

> . . . to be alone, walking in the fields and groves, and seems to have some one invisible always conversing with her.[42]

---

[40] Ibid., p. 88.
[41] Murray, *Jonathan Edwards*, p. 92.
[42] Ibid.

Thirteen-year-olds who are energized by being alone usually grow up to be adults who are energized by being alone. Where was that solitude for Sarah, a woman with a newborn every other year, with a steady stream of travelers and apprentices living in her house, and with a town who noticed every twitch of her life?

Sarah's life was different after these weeks—different in the ways you would expect after God has specially visited someone. Jesus said, "You will recognize them by their fruits" (Matthew 7:16). Jonathan said she exhibited

> a great meekness, gentleness, and benevolence of spirit and behaviour; and a great alteration in those things that formerly used to be the person's failings; seeming to be much overcome and swallowed up by the late great increase of grace, to the observation of those who are most conversant and most intimately acquainted.[43]

He also reassured his reader that she had not become too heavenly minded to be any earthly good.

> Oh how good, said the person once, is it to work for God in the day-time, and at night to lie down under his smiles! High experiences and religious affections in this person have not been attended with any disposition at all to neglect the necessary business of a secular calling . . . but worldly business has been attended with great alacrity, as part of the service of God: the person declaring that, it being done thus, it was found to be as good as prayer.[44]

Her changed life bore the fingerprint of God, not of psychological imbalance. It is clear that Jonathan agreed with her belief that she had encountered God:

> If such things are enthusiasm, and the fruits of a distempered brain, let my brain be evermore possessed of that happy distemper! If this be distraction, I pray God that the world of

[43] Edwards, *Thoughts on the Revival*, p. 378.
[44] Ibid.

mankind may be all seized with this benign, meek, beneficent, beatifical, glorious distraction![45]

## THE WILDERNESS

After more than twenty years, Jonathan was unjustly ousted from his church in Northampton. Until he had another position, they had to remain in Northampton. It doesn't require much effort to empathize with Sarah's emotional and financial stress. It would have been challenge enough to remain where her husband had been rejected. But in addition, there was no salary. So for one year Sarah lived in a hostile setting and managed their large household with no steady income.

In Stockbridge there was a community of Indians and a few whites. They were urgently searching for a pastor at the same time that Jonathan was seeking God's next step for his life. In 1750 the Edwardses moved to Stockbridge, out on the western side of Massachusetts, on the pioneer edge of the British fingerhold on the continent.

In 1871, *Harpers New Monthly Magazine* ran an article featuring Stockbridge. This was more than one hundred years after Edwards's death, and yet at the time of the article he had come to bear international esteem surpassed only by George Washington. Many paragraphs of this article described his noteworthy role in the history of the town of Stockbridge. And though decades had passed, they hadn't forgotten the Northampton controversy that led to Jonathan's call to Stockbridge.

> There succeeded to that vacant office in the wild woods one whose name is not only highly honored throughout this land, but better known and more honored abroad, perhaps, than that of any of our countrymen except Washington. As a preacher, a philosopher, and a person of devoted piety he is unsurpassed. . . . But . . . after a most successful ministry of more than 20 years, a controversy had arisen between him and his people, and they had thrust him out from them rudely and almost in disgrace. The subsequent adoption of his views, not only at Northampton but throughout the churches of New

---

[45] Ibid.

England, has abundantly vindicated his position in that lamentable controversy. . . .

He was not too great in his own estimation to accept the place now offered him [in the small outpost of Stockbridge]. . . .

Edwards was almost a thinking machine. . . . That a man thus thoughtful should yet be indifferent to many things of practical importance would not be strange. Accordingly we are told that the care of his domestic and secular affairs was devolved almost entirely upon his wife, who happily, while of kindred spirit with him in many respects, and fitted to be his companion, was also capable of assuming the cares which were thus laid upon her. It is said that Edwards did not know his own cows, nor even how many belonged to him. About all the connection he had with them seems to have been involved in the act of driving them to and from pasture occasionally, which he was willing to do for the sake of needful exercise. A story is told in this connection, which illustrates his obliviousness of small matters. As he was going for the cows once, a boy opened the gate for him with a respectful bow. Edwards acknowledged the kindness and asked the boy whose son he was. "Noah Clark's boy," was the reply. . . . On his return, the same boy . . . opened the gate for him again. Edwards [asked again who he was]. . . . "The same man's boy I was a quarter of an hour ago, Sir."[46]

## LAST CHAPTER

This was a family who had hardly tasted death, yet they were always aware of its constant nearness. How easily might a woman die in childbirth. How easily might a child die of fever. How easily might one be struck by gunshot or an arrow of war. How easily might a fireplace spark a house fire, with all asleep and lost.

When Jonathan wrote to his children, he often reminded them—not morbidly, but almost as a matter of fact—how close death might be. For Jonathan, the reality of death led automatically to the need for eternal life. He wrote to their ten-year-old Jonathan Jr. about the death of a playmate. "This is a loud call of God to you to prepare for death. . . .

---

[46] "A New England Village," *Harper's New Monthly Magazine*, November 1871, http://www.rootsweb.com/~maberksh/harpers/ (accessed 5-6-05).

Never give yourself any rest unless you have good evidence that you are converted and become a new creature."[47]

A family tragedy was the opening page of the final chapter of their lives.

Their daughter Esther was the wife of Aaron Burr, the president of the College of New Jersey, which would later be renamed Princeton. On September 24, 1757, this son-in-law of Jonathan and Sarah died suddenly, leaving Esther and two small children. This would be the first of five family deaths in a year.

Aaron Burr's death left the presidency open at the College of New Jersey, and Edwards was invited to become president of the college. Jonathan had been extremely productive in his thinking and writing during the six Stockbridge years; so it was not easy to leave. But in January 1758, he set off for Princeton, expecting his family to join him in the spring.

George Marsden pictures the moment:

> He left Sarah and his children in Stockbridge, as 17-year-old Susannah later reported, "as affectionately as if he should not come again." When he was outside the house, he turned and declared, "I commit you to God."[48]

Jonathan had hardly moved into the President's House in Princeton when he received news that his father had died. As Marsden says, "A great force in his life was finally gone, though the power of the personality had faded some years earlier."[49]

In this final chapter of Jonathan's and Sarah's lives, there are key moments that encapsulate and confirm God's work through Sarah Edwards in the main roles she had been given by him.

## 1. Sarah's Role as a Mother, with the Desire to Raise Godly Children

When Aaron Burr died, we catch a glimpse of how well the mother had prepared the daughter for unexpected tragedy. Esther wrote to her mother, Sarah, two weeks after he died:

---

[47] Marsden, *Jonathan Edwards*, p. 412.
[48] Ibid., p. 491.
[49] Ibid.

God has seemed sensibly near, in such a supporting and comfortable manner that I think I have never experienced the like. . . . I doubt not but I have your and my honoured father's prayers, daily, for me, but give me leave to entreat you to request earnestly of the Lord that I may never . . . faint under this his severe stroke. . . . O I am afraid I shall conduct myself so as to bring dishonour on . . . the religion which I profess.[50]

At the darkest moment of her life, Sarah's daughter fervently desired not to dishonor God.

## 2. Sarah's Role as the Wife of Jonathan

Soon after Jonathan arrived in Princeton, he was inoculated for smallpox. This was still an experimental procedure. He contracted the disease, and on March 22, 1758, he died, while Sarah was still back in Stockbridge, packing for the family's move to Princeton. Fewer than three months had passed since he had said good-bye at their doorstep. During the last minutes of his life, his thoughts and words were for his beloved wife. He whispered to one of his daughters:

It seems to me to be the will of God, that I must shortly leave you; therefore give my kindest love to my dear wife, and tell her, that the uncommon union, which has so long subsisted between us, has been of such a nature, as I trust is spiritual, and therefore will continue for ever: and I hope she will be supported under so great a trial, and submit cheerfully to the will of God.[51]

A week and a half later Sarah wrote to Esther (whose husband had died just six months earlier):

My very dear child, What shall I say? A holy and good God has covered us with a dark cloud. O that we may kiss the rod, and lay our hands upon our mouths! The Lord has done it. He has made me adore his goodness, that we had him so

---

[50] Dodds, *Marriage to a Difficult Man*, p. 160.
[51] Sereno E. Dwight, "Memoirs of Jonathan Edwards," in Edwards, *Works*, 1:clxxviii.

long. But my God lives; and he has my heart. O what a legacy my husband, and your father, has left us! We are all given to God; and there I am, and love to be.

Your affectionate mother,
Sarah Edwards[52]

Esther never read her mother's letter. On April 17, 1757, less than two weeks after her father's death, Esther died of a fever, leaving behind little Sally and Aaron Jr.[53] Sarah traveled to Princeton to stay with her grandchildren for a while and then take them back to Stockbridge with her.

## 3. Her Role as a Child of God

In October, Sarah was traveling toward Stockbridge with Esther's children. While stopping in the home of friends, she was overcome with dysentery and her life on earth ended. It was October 2, 1758, and she was forty-nine. The people with her reported that "she apprehended her death was near, when she expressed her entire resignation to God and her desire that he might be glorified in all things; and that she might be enabled to glorify him to the last; and continued in such a temper, calm and resigned, till she died."[54]

Sarah Edwards was the fifth family death in a year, and the fourth Edwards family grave added to the Princeton Cemetery during that fateful year, the end of the earthly lives of Jonathan and Sarah Edwards.

After more than 250 years, Jonathan Edwards remains America's greatest theologian and probably our greatest thinker. He has influenced our way of understanding the world and seeing God. Of course, that makes us curious about Sarah. How could she have known the gift she was giving us as she freed Jonathan to fulfill his calling?

But, as with any biography, we'd be wasting our time if we were satisfied just to nose around in their lives for interesting tidbits. So I have

---

[52] Ibid., 1:clxxix.

[53] Aaron Burr Jr. became vice president under President Thomas Jefferson. He fell into political and personal disfavor when he challenged Alexander Hamilton to a duel and killed him.

[54] Dodds, *Marriage to a Difficult Man*, p. 169.

prayed that this story would turn our eyes and affections toward biblical truth, that we would be edified and encouraged.

One way that happens in biography is by our recognizing something about ourselves in someone else's story. I see that Sarah Edwards was the wife of a pastor who was an intensely deep thinker with strong biblically based convictions. I see a woman who loved Romans 8:35: "Who shall separate us from the love of Christ?" I see something of myself in her life. And so, when she is faced with difficulties and challenges, I feel them more weightily, because they are something like the weights I carry. And I can see how God worked to lift the burdens for her, and therefore recognize it more clearly when he does it for me.

I see a woman who was probably fairly reserved and yet she was overtaken by an overwhelming spiritual experience that changed her life. I think my inclination, if I went through a similar two weeks, would be to play down the experience, to rationalize it away somehow—as the various biographers tried to do for Sarah. But I see Sarah looking to God for the explanation. As Colossians 3:16 says: "Let the word of Christ dwell in you richly, teaching and admonishing one another in all wisdom." I am admonished by Sarah's life.

Even more directly she admonished Samuel Hopkins when he was not correctly interpreting God's work in his life. I found this conversation to be a huge encouragement when I first read it in the midst of my mundane small-child-filled existence. We all have quiet conversations that might be forgotten. In the same way, Sarah's with Samuel would have been forgotten, except for Hopkins's journal. Their talk was part of a chain that led onward at least as far as Emerson and Thoreau, and *that* certainly wasn't the end of it—we just don't have the records of what happened next, and next, and next. We usually *don't* know how God winds the threads of our lives on and on and on.

I was also struck by the holy looseness with which Jonathan and Sarah held their children. In an age when death hovered so closely— from war, illness, wild animals, infection, childbirth, and injury—I would expect parents to grasp their children tightly to them, to keep them always in sight. On the contrary, Jonathan and Sarah, already living in Stockbridge on the treacherous edge of the wilderness, allowed their ten-year-old Jonathan Jr. to travel with an evangelist even further west on a mission to Indians in the mountains—their *ten*-year-old!

This didn't mean they were ignorant of the perils. This was the time that Jonathan wrote to Jonathan Jr. about the death of a playmate. "This is a loud call of God to you to prepare for death. . . . Never give yourself any rest unless you have good evidence that you are converted and become a new creature."[55] No, they were all too aware of the nearness of physical death. But the death of the body was not what called forth prayers for and pleas to their children. The imminence of physical death made them fear not the removal of life, but the absence of life eternal. This is a perspective I want to have toward the ones I love.

Sarah Edwards was the supporter and protector and homebuilder for Jonathan Edwards, whose philosophy and passion for God is vital still three hundred years after his birth. She was the godly mother and example to eleven children who became the parents of outstanding citizens of this country, and—immensely more important to her—many are also citizens of heaven. She was the hostess and comforter and encourager of Samuel Hopkins, and who knows how many others, who went on to minister to others, who went on to minister to others, who went on . . . She was an example to George Whitefield, and who knows how many others, of a godly wife.

At the heart of everything, she was a child of God, who from early years experienced sweet, spiritual communion with him, and who over the years grew in grace, and who, at least once, was very dramatically visited by God in a way that changed her life.

*Just as Sarah Edwards had little idea of the ongoing generations she would influence through her interaction with Samuel Hopkins, there are two women who probably have little notion of their impact on me and therefore also on my husband, children, friends, and church. Long before my husband was called to a pulpit ministry, I admired our pastors' wives, one in California, one in Minnesota. God used them to help prepare me for my future role that none of us yet expected. And so this story of Sarah Edwards is dedicated to Delores Hoeldtke and Anne Ortlund.*

---

[55] Marsden, *Jonathan Edwards*, p. 412.

$B$ut [God] said to me, "My grace is sufficient for you,
for my power is made perfect in weakness."
Therefore I will boast all the more gladly of my weaknesses,
so that the power of Christ may rest upon me.
For the sake of Christ, then, I am content with weaknesses,
insults, hardships, persecutions, and calamities.
For when I am weak, then I am strong.

2 CORINTHIANS 12:9-10


$H$ave you not known? Have you not heard?
The LORD is the everlasting God,
the Creator of the ends of the earth.
He does not faint or grow weary;
his understanding is unsearchable.
He gives power to the faint,
and to him who has no might he increases strength.
Even youths shall faint and be weary,
and young men shall fall exhausted;
but they who wait for the LORD shall renew their strength;
they shall mount up with wings like eagles;
they shall run and not be weary;
they shall walk and not faint.

ISAIAH 40:28-31

# LILIAS TROTTER

## *Faithful in Weakness*

In A.D. 354, if you had traveled a thousand miles almost due south from London—which at the time was a bustling settlement ruled by Rome and called Londinium—you would have traversed the land of the Franks and come to the Great Sea. After you crossed the Mediterranean, your first landfall would have been the land that is now Algeria. At the time, it was Numidia, a province of the Roman Empire. In that year, in a small town a few miles inland, a farmer and his wife had a baby boy. They named him Aurelius Augustinus. We know him as St. Augustine, one of the giants of church history.

During his years as Bishop of Hippo (now Annaba, Algeria), the Roman Empire began its fall into ruin. Augustine died as the ravaging Vandals moved into his land. After the Vandals came the Byzantine Empire. Then in the 600s came the Arabs from the East, bringing Islam and Arabic language and culture. From the 1500s until the early 1800s, the Ottoman Empire strengthened the hold of Islam on this area. By the time the French gained control of Algeria in 1830, the Christian church had disappeared.

Fifteen hundred years after Augustine's birth, twelve hundred years after the great Arab migration westward, and twenty-three years after the French invasion, Algeria was far from the thoughts of Alexander and Isabella Trotter on July 14, 1853, when their daughter Isabella Lilias was born. They would not live to see Algeria take its place of importance in Lilias's life.

Alexander Trotter was a respected stockbroker. He was known to his family as having a "charming character of love, gentleness, generosity and unselfishness."[56] He exhibited respect for people from

---

[56] The impressions of Alexander and Isabella Rockness are drawn from Miriam Huffman Rockness, *A Passion for the Impossible: The Life of Lilias Trotter* (Wheaton, Ill., Harold Shaw Publishers, 1999), chapter 2. In writing this chapter, I have depended heavily on this excellent biography, which includes a helpful bibliography of works by and about Lilias Trotter. I am extremely grateful to Miriam Rockness for her research, skill, and interest in Lilias Trotter. A newer edition is available (Grand Rapids: Discovery House Publishers, 2003).

widely different ranks in life, which led him to express his Christian faith with a "special concern for the condition of public institutions," such as prisons, poorhouses, and orphanages. He loved new experiences and was fascinated by the wonders of the natural world, examined in person or through the scientific journals he enjoyed. Lilias and her siblings remembered his helping them with experiments at home and taking them to scientific exhibits and lectures.

Decades later, in Algiers, Lilias wrote of her father with affection. After she had placed something for safekeeping in her bedside table, she wrote:

> This is lying beside me in the drawer of what used to be the table of my father's dressing room—the drawer he used to call my garden, the other one alongside being Alec's [her brother]. He used to hide in our respective gardens any little gifts, picture-books, or toys that he had picked up on his way from the City.[57]

Isabella Trotter, Lilias's mother, was interested in a wide range of topics, from gardening and decorating to geology and botany. "Her sympathetic nature made her a stout advocate for the disadvantaged . . . and it was that same natural concern for others that was evidenced in subsequent years by her daughter."[58] In Isabella's letters are descriptions and a heart for beauty that reappear later in Lilias's writings. Mrs. Trotter held strongly to her Christian faith and belief, though her parents and other wider family circle were more "open-minded and tolerant." She seems to have been more spontaneous than her husband and less scientifically oriented. Once when she and Alexander were on a trip away from home, she wrote her children about a playful argument over the length of a comet's tail: "I say it looks two yards long, but Papa says it is difficult to tell this, but that it is really about a degree and a half in length, or about six diameters of the moon."[59]

---

[57] Blanche A. F. Pigott, I, Lilias Trotter (London: Marshall, Morgan & Scott Ltd., nd), p. 211. (The book was apparently written in 1929; see footnote, p. 32 of Pigott's book.) Blanche Pigott was a long-time friend of Lilias Trotter. The book is taken primarily from Trotter's journals and letters. Pigott describes their first interaction, after one of the Higher Life Conferences:

We walked across the Park to the edge of the wood. . . . I had come to the turning of the ways in my life, and was sorely perplexed, realizing that to follow what I felt was God's will for me would be the breaking of the most precious ties. I told her my difficulty, and in great distress, cried, "What must I do?" Without hesitation she answered, "You can only obey God."

[58] Rockness, A Passion for the Impossible, p. 29.
[59] Ibid., p. 35.

Lilias's father died when she was twelve. Her family saw a distinct change in her as she learned to lean on her heavenly Father now that her papa, Alexander, was gone. Sometimes when they expected to find her playing, they would find her instead praying in her room. The personalities, faith, interests, and personal qualities of Alexander and Isabella were strongly reflected in their daughter Lilias as she matured. Her father died too early to have seen the woman she became. But her mother apparently approved of the life of ministry that Lilias moved into. And Isabella encouraged Lilias's extraordinary natural artistic gift. The only relics from Lilias's childhood are a drawing and sketchbook given her by her mother—a symbol, perhaps, of that encouragement of Lilias's eye for beauty and artistic ability.[60]

## MOVING INTO MINISTRY

When Lilias was nineteen, she and her mother attended their first Higher Life Conference—the precursor of today's Keswick Ministries.[61] After that, she attended almost every year, and the conferences had a strong influence in deepening Lilias's spiritual life. In years to come, Keswick friends would provide significant support and personnel for the ministry God would lead her into.

Each year, following the conference, Lilias was involved with the local missions outreaches arranged by the conference organizers. For example, her sister writes in a letter about helping serve a late-night supper for omnibus men, the hard-working drivers of horse-drawn "buses":

> What do you think L[ilias] and I were about from half-past ten last night till 3 a.m.? A rare good time it was. It was a very wet night, but they came about 180 in number; some could not arrive till 1 a.m. They had a splendid supper, quantities of singing, very short telling addresses. I do trust there may have been much blessing; many of them never go anywhere.[62]

During these ministry years in the 1870s, Dwight L. Moody held four annual great campaigns in London. As a member of the volunteer

---

[60] Ibid., p. 31.

[61] Keswick continues as a multi-faceted international ministry maintaining its original goal of deepening the spiritual life of individuals and churches. Its headquarters is in England.

[62] Pigott, *I, Lilias Trotter*, p. 5.

force for the campaigns, Lilias received training from Moody himself about how to talk to people who were seeking and inquiring after God. Only recently, Moody had begun using the *Wordless Book*.[63] It's likely that Lilias was introduced by Moody to this evangelistic tool. In Algeria years later, Lilias mentions the *Wordless Book*, especially where language was a barrier.[64] But in 1875, she had no inkling that this evangelism training was preparation for missions, because as yet missions meant nothing to her.

Her outreach experiences served as steppingstones into what nowadays we would call "inner-city ministry" in London. She was active at the Welbeck Street Institute, a sort of hostel that provided housing and food for poor women who needed help.

## TWO CONSUMING PASSIONS

In 1876, when Lilias was twenty-three, she traveled in Europe with her mother and sister. At her first sight of the snowy alps, "she was so overcome by their majestic beauty that she burst into tears."[65] A trip like this filled her sensitive eye and soul with color and light that her skillful hand and brush released onto her sketch pad.

Two momentous friendships began during this trip. First, at a convention in Switzerland, she met Blanche Haworth, who became a close friend and in a decade would become her missions partner and closest friend.

Then in Venice, Mrs. Trotter discovered that John Ruskin was staying in the same hotel. Ruskin was an "artist, critic, social philosopher and a towering figure in Victorian England."[66] He was *the* voice of the art world of his day. If he said something was good, it was good. Mrs. Trotter sent him a packet of Lilias's watercolors and a note: "Mrs. Alex Trotter has the pleasure of sending Professor Ruskin her daughter's water-colors. Mrs. Trotter is quite prepared to hear that he does not approve of them—she has drawn from childhood and has had very lit-

---

[63] Charles Spurgeon introduced the concept—his book had only black, red, and white pages, symbolizing the sinner's need for salvation, the provision of Christ's blood for atonement, and the redeemed's resulting purity—in a sermon in 1866. Subsequently other pages were added by others. Nine years after Spurgeon's sermon, Moody began to use the Wordless Book. http://www.virtualservant.org/cef/wordlessbook/ (accessed 2/13/05).

[64] Rockness, *A Passion for the Impossible*, p. 104.

[65] Piggot, p. 9.

[66] Miriam Rockness, "Lilias Trotter: Almost Famous," *Victoria*, July 2001, p. 22.

tle teaching. But if Mrs. Trotter could have Mr. Ruskin's opinion it would be most valuable."[67]

Though Lilias was moved easily to tears by beauty and loved to paint, it was true that she had received no formal art training. Her skill was a gift. Her sister remembered with ironic amusement: "Of drawing lessons she fortunately had only one short course in landscape—indoors—from which no benefit was derived."[68]

Ruskin described the watercolors he received as "extremely right-minded and careful work."[69] Although the words sound measured, his response reflected more animation. He showed the Trotters the art treasures of Venice, gave Lilias drawing assignments, and invited her to be his student when she returned to England. He took her under his wing, tutoring her and foreseeing for her a great future as a world-class artist. She and her sister visited him often at his home in the Lake District, where he helped Lilias refine her skill. These weeks immersed in color and form and beauty offered rejuvenation to the spirit of this young woman who spent the rest of her time in the dimmest districts of London.

But by the time Lilias was twenty-six, Ruskin became frustrated with her for letting herself be distracted from her art. He didn't approve of the way she was dividing her weeks. She was spending far too much time in the streets of London and not enough with her paints. So Ruskin laid out for her the glory of the life of art that lay before her. If she would devote herself to art, he said, "she would be the greatest living painter and do things that would be immortal."[70]

This was an agonizing decision. Running parallel in her life were *two* all-consuming passions—art and ministry. She knew it isn't possible to be wholly consumed twice. It is not possible to give yourself *totally* to two different masters. But, she came to see, it *is* possible that one of the passions could become servant to the other. Still, she had to decide which passion would become the master of the other.

For several days, Lilias weighed her desires and prayed for God to make his calling clear. Her friend Blanche Pigott wrote,

---

[67] Ibid., p. 22.
[68] Pigott, p. 4.
[69] Rockness, "Almost Famous," p. 22.
[70] Rockness, *A Passion for the Impossible*, p. 68.

She told me that she felt as if she had lived years in those few days.

In writing to me . . . she says, . . . "You will understand that it is not from vanity I tell you [the compliments Ruskin paid her work], at least I think not, because I know that I have no more to do with the gift than with the colour of my hair—but because I need prayer to see clearly God's way." The intense delight she felt . . . at the prospect of a life given to Art and surrounded by Art only made her seek all the more earnestly to be guided by God's will alone.[71]

She loved her art and knew it was possible that God could use her influence in that sphere for his Kingdom's purposes. But in the end she said, "I see as clear as daylight now, I cannot give myself to painting in the way he [Ruskin] means and continue still to 'seek first the Kingdom of God and His Righteousness.'"[72]

She was free now to throw herself wholeheartedly into her ministry in London. She remained Ruskin's friend to the end of his life, though he never understood her decision. And she still loved art—how could she *not* when her soul was so tenderly vulnerable to beauty. But she enjoyed her art now as a gift, not a passion. Much later, she realized even more strongly the importance of focusing on Jesus, rather than on all the good things he gives us.

Never has it been so easy to live in half a dozen good harmless worlds at once—art, music, social science, games, motoring, the following of some profession, and so on. And between them we run the risk of drifting about, the "good" hiding the "best.". . .

It is easy to find out whether our lives are focussed, and if so, where the focus lies. Where do our thoughts settle when consciousness comes back in the morning? Where do they swing back when the pressure is off during the day? . . . Dare to have it out with God . . . and ask Him to show you whether or not all is focussed on Christ and His glory. . . .

How do we bring things to a focus in the world of optics?

[71] Pigott, pp. 9-10.
[72] Ibid., p. 11.

Not by looking at the things to be dropped, but by looking at the one point that is to be brought out. Turn your soul's vision to Jesus, and look and look at Him, and a strange dimness will come over all that is apart from Him.[73]

## MINISTRY AND PERSONAL LIFE

For more than ten years, Lilias worked with the Welbeck Street Institute, continuing with it through its merger with some other organizations to form the first YWCA. The goals at Welbeck blended well with the aim of the newly created YWCA to "unite young women in prayer and evangelism, to promote Christian friendship and mutual help, and to promote the moral, social, and cultural well-being of its members."[74]

For Lilias the ministry meant helping to create and run places and programs for poor working girls to get meals and to sleep. It meant teaching Bible classes for women and children. And she was involved in rescue work, which meant being wherever women needed help getting out of bad situations, perhaps "sitting up all night with a poor half-crazed girl, to save her from threatened suicide;"[75] or perhaps going out on the street to offer prostitutes a safe place.

> For many young girls stranded in the city without skills or means of employment [prostitution] was a tragic recourse. . . . Lilias fearlessly traversed the streets to rescue these street-walkers. . . . She brought them back to the hostel for a good night's sleep and for training in an employable skill, and she introduced them to the Good Shepherd.[76]

Lilias's ministry choices had fairly direct implications in her personal life. Victorian England was layered by a very distinct sense of class. By choosing to work among what was considered to be the lowest people in society, she was cutting herself off from friendships among fashionable society. In the first place, proper ladies did not "work." And they certainly didn't walk out alone or frequent those

[73] Rockness, *A Passion for the Impossible*, pp. 288-289.
[74] Ibid., p 73.
[75] Pigott, p. 15.
[76] Rockness, *A Passion for the Impossible*, p. 75.

parts of town. Mothers in the level of society into which Lilias was born would not have wanted for their sons a woman who behaved in such an unseemly manner. In effect, Lilias was choosing to remain single.

## A BROADER VISION

In 1884—when Lilias was about twenty-nine—she underwent some slight surgery. She was so exhausted beforehand that the recuperation at home was long. She missed weeks of her work at the YWCA. And she was left with a permanently damaged heart. But even a weak heart that would have turned many women into semi-invalids couldn't keep her at home. As she returned to her ministry, God was preparing a broader vision for her.

> I was busy in London working; all was prospering, with God's blessing, and I had no thought but to spend my life there. The whole missionary subject seemed to me rather dull, and was altogether beyond my horizon. But I had two friends with whom I was thrown a good deal just then, and they had both of them taken to heart the outer darkness [areas of the world that were unreached with the gospel]. I do not remember that they said anything to me personally about it, but one felt it right through them; they were all aglow, and after a bit, though I took no more personal interest in the matter than before, I began to feel they had a fellowship with Jesus that I knew nothing about. I did love Him, and I did not like to be out in the cold over it, so I began to pray: "Lord give me the fellowship with Thee about the [unreached peoples] that Thou has given to those two."
>
> It was not many weeks before it began to come—a strange yearning love over those who were "in the land of the shadow of death," a feeling that Jesus could speak to me about it, and that I could speak to Him; that a great barrier between me and Him had been broken down, and swept away. I had no thought of leaving England then, no thought even at first of trying to stir others at home, but straight as a line God made my way out into the darkness [to the mission field where he was leading her], before eighteen months were over.[77]

---

77 Pigott, p. 84.

Two things began to happen. First, she began to feel a yearning toward the needs of faraway, non-Christian lands. Second, as one of her friends said, "She told me that whenever she prayed, the words 'North Africa' sounded in her soul as though a voice were calling her."[78]

It didn't really seem possible that she could go anywhere, though, because she was committed to caring for Jaqueline, her invalid sister, for six months each year, their mother having died a few years earlier.

Then, in May 1887, she heard a missionary speaker say that just four days before, he had been in Algeria, North Africa. She said, "In that first sentence God's call had sounded. If Algeria was so near as that, I could spend half the year there and the other half at home, then it was for me, and before morning there remained no shadow of a doubt that it was his plan."[79]

On her thirty-fourth birthday, July 14, 1887, she sent an application to North African Mission. They didn't think it wise to accept responsibility for her, because her weak heart kept her from passing their health exam. They were willing, though, for her to "work in harmony with this mission, but not connected to it."[80]

## ALGERIA

So Lilias Trotter launched out on March 5, 1888, with, as she said, "a strange glad feeling of utter loosing and being cast upon God."[81] Her companions were Lucy Lewis and Blanche Haworth, who had been a special friend since they met in Switzerland. Blanche would be Lilias's constant co-worker and closest friend for thirty years, as others came and went.

The women left England less than nine months after Lilias had sensed God's call. Most contemporary missionaries would confirm that as not nearly enough preparation time. But actually she had undergone thirty-four years of preparation. God doesn't waste anything, and her whole life so far had prepared her to do missions in ways that wouldn't have been thought of by missions training programs available to her.

The women sailed into Algiers on March 9, 1888. This small team of missionaries brought a boatload of obstacles with them.

---

[78] Ibid., p. 15.
[79] Rockness, *A Passion for the Impossible*, p. 79.
[80] Ibid., p. 80.
[81] Ibid.

Not one of them was fit to pass a medical exam for any mission society. . . . The three women knew neither a living soul in Algeria nor a sentence of Arabic. They had not a clue for beginning a work in untouched ground.[82]

If God works through the weakness of humans, as Lilias believed, he had it here in full force!

They began to pray the threefold prayer that would be their heart's cry for years to come: that doors might be opened, that hearts might be opened, and that the heavens might be opened. Then simply by taking each practical step before them, they faced the barriers between them and the people.

The greatest barrier was Islam. The religious observance of Islam required then, as now, five duties called *The Pillars of Islam*: confession of faith, prayer in Arabic five times daily, fasting during the thirty days of Ramadan, almsgiving, and pilgrimage to Mecca or other holy places. These observances were woven into the daily life and culture but did little to change lives.

Just weeks after her arrival, Lilias received word of the death of her invalid sister. This was a blow. Lilias's plan had been to divide each year in half, between missions in Algeria and care for Jaqueline. So when Lilias had said good-bye to Jaqueline, she expected to see her again in six months. Lucy and Blanche were with her to help her feel God's comfort in her grief.

We were just going to church when the letters came. They made me wait for half an hour, and then we went in time for the Communion Service. It was so beautiful to go straight to that before anything of realization came; it has been a help having all the household work to do, as the bodily tiredness made one sleep. God has been very good.[83]

And now Lilias found she was released to focus wholly on Algeria.

---

[82] Ibid., p. 87.
[83] Pigott, p. 23.

## LANGUAGE AND LIVING

Their first task was to learn Arabic. Nowadays missionaries may take classes that teach them how to learn a new language. Lilias and her co-workers had to make up their own methods, using the resources at hand. Their first effort was to write down the Gospel of John word for word in Arabic, going from English to French to Arabic, because a French-Arabic dictionary was the translation tool they had. They attended Arabic classes until the teacher got sick and quit. A young boy met with them three times a week until he got scared and didn't return. After a few months, they hired a professional tutor. "Oh we do so long to speak," Lilias writes. "The power of talking can only come by being among the people—but time will shew God's plan."[84]

Though their goal was to live with and minister among Arabs, the women set up their first household in the French quarter of the city, because they could speak French. (Algeria was a French colony all of their years there.) When they first arrived, they were eager to meet anyone who was willing to spend time with them. Some of their earliest contacts were with French-speaking neighbors, whom the women invited to regular Sunday meetings in their home.

Even before they knew much Arabic, they had their tutor translate small portions of Scripture into Arabic, which they printed as decorative cards. They took these to the Arab part of town to distribute, to open conversation with Arab men who could speak French. In cafés sometimes the waiters would read the verses aloud to all the customers. At the waterfront, the women distributed cards in several languages to the seamen from many nations. Along the way there were growing opportunities for the women to practice Arabic.

## ARAB WOMEN

But still there was no easy way to get to Arab women. Although many men knew French, the women, on the whole, knew only Arabic. Until Lilias and her co-workers learned the language, there was no easy way to communicate with most of the local women.

Another barrier was that the women were usually secluded in their homes. An Arab woman belonged to her father until marriage, and then to her husband. Her life was to serve first the one, then the other.

---

[84] Rockness, *A Passion for the Impossible,* p. 89.

After about age ten, a girl was veiled and separated from any contact with men.

Then as now, usually a woman would be the one who could reach a woman—if she were welcome in a home. Children often were the entry key. When the English women befriended a child on the doorstep, the child might take them inside to his mother.

Lilias described the scene that they would find as they entered a typical Arab house beside a winding, narrow alleyway in the old Arab city, the Casbah. The courtyard would be small, no benches, no greenery, lots of people, and scattered cooking utensils—rundown and confused:

> The women all mix freely, and do their cooking together in the court on the lower floor, but if a man comes in, he clears his throat violently in the little vestibule inside the street door, and instantly all the women and girls run helter-skelter into their rooms, like rabbits to their holes, and pull down the door curtains, and the place is cleared of all except his own women, for they recognize the throat of their lord and master. As soon as he has passed in his room, they all pop out again. In every house there are four or five families, and in the lease of a room it is entered that unless in illness or urgent need, the men must not come in between 7 am and 7 pm, except for their midday meal, which leaves the ground much freer for us.[85]

The greatest obstacle was that the message of the gospel was inconceivable.

> We talked to one [woman] who could speak French; we began speaking of our Lord's love; she shook her head most sadly. "No, He does not love the women, only the men." We repeated John 3:16. But she only said again and again, "No, no, not the world, not the women."[86]

Later, when prayers were answered and one woman did become a Christian, there were cultural barriers to overcome. The woman wanted to obey Scripture and be baptized, but there was a problem.

---

[85] Pigott, pp. 32-33.
[86] Ibid., p. 21.

The difficulty was that the women could not bear the thought of being touched by a strange man. "It is sin—It is impossible," they said to the missionaries. . . . So they prayed on, and to their joy found that the woman's Christian husband was willing for her to be baptized by Mr. Brading, a missionary with whom they were in fellowship. It was a sore point with the woman, but at last she yielded.[87]

From the beginning, Lilias felt a special calling to the women, and that burden never lifted. Through the years she dreamed of ways to reach them. She knew there was not just one all-purpose strategy that would accomplish this. She and her co-workers visited women in their homes. They developed embroidery and Bible classes for girls and women. On the rare days when women left their homes, usually for a ceremony at the graves of relatives, the European women rented a room for an "open house" where the local women could relax and socialize away from home.

Although almost all the Muslim women were illiterate, Lilias became especially concerned that there be strong Christian literature for them, looking forward to the day when girls would receive an education. Later, in 1909, when changes were happening in the society, she could see that dawn on the horizon. She wrote to fellow workers across North Africa:

New literature for Christian women. Do fellow-missionaries sigh over the words, and think it is a far day to the need for that? It may not be. We have a God who lives in eternity, and knows no time-limits. We can be getting ready for the showers, like the autumn crocus of these southern lands, that rears its head in faith, while, as yet, there is hardly a cloud in the sky. . . .

Pray for intelligent Christian women to be raised up by God from among themselves, who will interpret to us the half-explored mentality and the half-realized life conditions that we seek to reach.

And do not let us feel "it is all premature." Faith is generally premature; it deals with "things not seen as yet." For us

---

[87] I. R. Govan Stewart, *The Love That Was Stronger* (London: Lutterworth Press, 1958), p. 35.

vision on this point has almost begun. Do not let us lose our last chance of believing by waiting till the dawn has broken into the day.[88]

## THE SOUTHLANDS

In March 1893, when Lilias was almost forty, she and Blanche made their first expedition into the desert, to Biskra, about 250 miles south of Algiers. Today the cities are connected by a highway. For them it was a 288-mile train ride east to Constantine, then south 150 miles by horse-drawn wagon to El Kantara, and then 30 miles by camel.

Her verbal visions of these lands make clear her love of the desert and prove that her pen was as descriptive and delicate as her paintbrush. And her eye for beauty remained bright. Waking one morning in the desert, she wrote this journal entry in 1914, twenty-six years after she left her artistic career.

> Sunrise came with great scarab wings of dusty red behind the purple mountains. On the other side the hills stood in madder [reddish orange] against a sky of cloisonné blue. . . . A bit longer and the scarab wings had got glorified into white pinions of all the hosts of heaven all against a sky of tenderest shades of turquoise, melting to indescribable green and mauve as it neared the horizon.[89]

Lilias's dream was to create outposts for the gospel in outlying desert towns. She hoped that someday there would be Christians to live and minister there permanently. But in the meantime she hoped she and her co-workers could visit periodically. In a desert town, sometimes she would simply walk along the dusty lane, stopping at doors to see where she might be welcome. Often the desert women would invite her in and call their friends to visit too.

> One of them showed me scratches on her face made when mourning for her husband who died a few days ago. "What do you do when people die?" she asked. I told her that if we believed in Jesus, God comforted us. It seemed to strike them

---

[88] Pigott, p. 136.
[89] Ibid., p. 153.

so, they kept repeating it to one another, "God comforts them! God comforts them!"[90]

Lilias was not daunted by the traveling conditions. Each journey was risky for two women traveling alone with an unfamiliar guide through territories where Europeans were targets for desert bandits, scorpions, disease, and ferocious dogs. There were no roads through the great, constantly shifting sand dunes, which rose up to 400 feet above the floor. A sandstorm would cover the subtle markings on the way. Even tiny miscalculations could mean missing a destination by miles. Within hours, the air could sear the lungs and the sun burn the traveler. It could take only half a day to reach dehydration.

> It was a broiling sun on the march, and Blanche had the near-est escape of a sunstroke, which gave her days of agonizing headache and fever pains. We eagerly watched the line of palms getting nearer, and made straight for a palm pit. . . . The only coolness to be found was plunging our hands into the sand; it felt a little cool, though when we took its temperature, for curiosity, it proved to be 88 degrees.[91]

Travel was painfully slow. It could take days of slogging through the sand to go just a couple of hundred miles. Even today in the first years of the twenty-first century, it's not hard to find people in North African countries who remember the three-day trip by camel to a city that can be reached now in two hours by car on an expressway.

In modern Algeria there are bus routes and trains and highways between towns. For Lilias there was nothing but camel, horse, and carriage. And Lilias loved it.

> Oh, the desert is lovely in its restfulness—the great brooding stillness over and through everything is so full of God. One does not wonder that he used to take his people out into the wilderness to teach them.[92]

A friend said it was never hard for Lilias to set out on a journey.

[90] Ibid., p. 43.
[91] Ibid., p. 65.
[92] Rockness, *A Passion for the Impossible*, p. 110.

The yearning to return to the desert was so great that she had to remind herself sometimes that it might be a temptation rather than a call of God:

> Such a cry has awakened these last days to get down to the desert again . . . a great deal of attraction to all that. . . . I don't suppose He can let me go until it has been dealt with and supplanted with a fellowship with Himself about these places.[93]

## MOVING TO THE ARAB QUARTER

In 1893, five years after coming to Algeria, Lilias and Blanche and their co-workers finally were able to move into a house in the Arab Quarter—an area most would have considered a slum. She wrote in a letter:

> It was good to turn our backs on the long French streets and plunge down among the crowds. [At the moment of crossing the threshold] came the word, "In this place I will give peace, saith the Lord.". . . On Sunday, when I nodded to them from my window, one called out to another, "They are the people who have harps!" I fetched my little zither harp . . . and they crept along a parapet . . . to a projection opposite my window where we could easily touch hands across the narrow street. There they sat, half a dozen women and girls against the sunset background, while we played and talked to them; then there was the sound of a man's voice in the street below and they crept back without another word.[94]

Six years later when an English friend was planning to visit and hoped to stay at Lilias's house, Lilias felt she should prepare her friend for a very non-English place. So for the first time she let herself describe the house through European eyes.

> Our spare room is dark and cheerless, and only fit to be inhabited for a few days, sun and light being essential here to health. Moreover an Arab house in the native quarter is not what the

doctors mean when they say, "Go to Algiers [for your health]."
The air here is so . . . generally breathed up and bad; even other
missionaries who come all say they are thankful they do not
live here. The house is both damp and draughty. Till the real
spring comes, the court, on to which all the rooms open, is
drenched whenever it rains, and there are no fireplaces.[95]

Children moved in and out of their home, especially under the care
of Blanche—the "Martha" of the pair. They made friends with neighborhood women, some of whom were inclined toward the gospel.

## SKIES OF BRASS

The opposition was great, though. As the women became fluent in
Arabic and more aware of the intricacies of the culture around them,
so too the evil became more obvious.

> More than ever . . . we have sights of the deliberate power of
> the devil around us. The moral filth that lies on all sides comes
> into view in directions we had never imagined, even right
> down among the small children; they are sunk in it. All the
> outward ways in which the powers of evil are invoked—the
> spells, the sorceries, and witchcraft—come to light more and
> more as we get contact with the people. No wonder that the
> very air seems impregnated with devilry, and that the sense of
> knowing him as the adversary has been keener than ever
> before, and a counter-move ready for every move God makes.
> More and more we come across strange, weird cases of illness
> brought on by anger, which seem more like cases of posses-
> sion than anything else.[96]

Sometimes the sense of oppression was so great that, as Lilias
wrote,

> One could literally do nothing but pray at every available bit;
> one might take up letters or accounts that seemed as if they
> were a "must be"—but one had to drop them within five min-

---

[95] Ibid., p. 85.
[96] Ibid., p. 97.

utes, almost invariably, and get to prayer—hardly prayer either—but a dumb crying up to skies of brass.[97]

Too many times they saw a newer convert begin to pull away and turn against them. They came to recognize the work of drugs, administered secretly in food or drink, which made the person open to suggestion and evil influences. As difficult as it was to see new saints die, the women found comfort in the knowledge that this was one way God protected his sheep.

> Roukia's brother-in-law has gone home in great peace. With his failing breath, hardly able to articulate the words, he repeated over and over, "I love Jesus a thousand times a thousand times." Then as the end came, with a wonderful shining in his face, "The gate of heaven is open—I enter in—Jesus," and he was gone.
>
> It is better so—oh, infinitely better! It used to make me sad when God saved them just to die. Now I can only rejoice that their training for the work of eternity is being carried on by God Himself, in the quiet of His haven. . . .[98]

## PATTERNS OF LIFE AND MINISTRY

Over the years, there were certain regular occurrences that gave a pattern to the ministry.

In the spring and sometimes in the fall, there might be an expedition to outlying villages to make new contacts for the gospel or to renew what had been done before.

In the beastliest summer, Lilias and her European co-workers usually spent some time in Europe for a time of refreshment and keeping their supporters connected with their work.

Each year Ramadan, the Muslim month of fasting, was a time of intense spiritual warfare for Lilias and her team. It was the season of greatest challenge for new Christians. Since keeping the fast was a main way of proving one's adherence to Islam, the Christians felt they should not keep the fast. This subjected them to harassment and persecution. Lilias and the other missionaries prayed intensely, offered a place

---

[97] Ibid., pp. 77-78.
[98] Ibid., p. 100.

where Christians could eat together, and eventually created a service of Communion during the Ramadan season.

> The Ramadan Communion Service is always a test time—will they or will they not dare to stand up in the face of the "adherents," who will doubtless spread the news? "Take, eat," is defiance of all the Moslem world.[99]

Another pattern for Lilias was created by her health. Every few years, after becoming more and more heavily involved in more and more ministry, she would suffer a physical breakdown. This would require her to extend her annual time in England.

Should she have been doing things differently? It's difficult and probably unfair to judge from this remove. We do know that in Algeria, she disciplined herself to take regular time away, hidden in the tufts of tall grass on a certain quiet hillside, for instance, to be alone with God. She was careful to take a break during the dangerously hot summer months and sometimes took a retreat in a seaside town away from Algiers.

But she was a woman who couldn't pass a mission physical. With her weak heart, it probably would not have seemed odd to most people if she had whiled away her life in England as a semi-invalid. Yes, her health periodically did require her to pull back and spend weeks or months of recuperation. But she did not live the life of a frail person. On the contrary, for the sake of the gospel, she was a pioneer in a land whose climate has broken the health of many who went out stronger than she was.

## PIONEER

Her pioneering spirit shone in her private life as well as in her ministry. In fact, that adventurous spirit may have accelerated her recuperation periods. In 1900, at the age of forty-seven, she began to experiment with technology—her new Brownie, a camera. That was the same year that she tried to learn to ski.

> We have taken to skiing for exercise. It looks delightfully like flying when you have got past the preliminaries of getting tan-

---

[99] Ibid., p. 216.

gled up in your six-foot shoes. Margaret [her sister] may arrive at it before she leaves, but I don't suppose I shall.[100]

Yes, Lilias periodically was kept from her place of mission by health, and also sometimes by the policies of the occupying French government. Was that wasted time? Did her "down" times hinder the gospel? Probably not. She accomplished more than most of us ever hope to. And it often seemed that the times of extra rest came just before a time of great difficulty and challenge—as if God were "charging her up."

And the times of resting were often rich in writing and creativity. Throughout Lilias Trotter's life, much of her evangelistic writing was done during the periods of rest and recuperation following a health breakdown. She seemed to see everything around her as a picture of God and his ways—as a parable. She compiled some of her parables into books during her illnesses. Nature was filled with lessons about its Creator.

> "I am come into deep waters" took on a new meaning this morning. . . . It dawned that shallow waters were a place where you can neither sink nor swim. In deep waters it is either the one or the other. . . . Swimming is the intensest, most strenuous form of motion. All of you is involved in it, and yet every inch of you is in abandonment of rest upon the water that bears you up. "We rest on Thee and in Thy name we go."[101]

Her journals were a combination of words, paintings, and sketches. Over time, she used many of the pictures to illustrate devotional books that gave thousands of people a glimpse of real life in an area that seemed at the time remote and exotic. Today her paintings would serve as a vivid history of desert and Arab peoples and places that now are in the center of our contemporary world's awareness. But unfortunately her art is inaccessible, stored away in archives in England—until a wise and daring publisher is willing to make them available again.[102]

---

[100] Ibid., p. 89.

[101] Ibid., p. 239.

[102] "Lilias had preserved 'thirty litle diary volumes.' Where were they? . . . My search took me . . . to Loughborough, England, and the office of Arab World Ministries. . . . There I was amazed to discover her archives: a rich reservoir of books, leaflets and, most compellingly, her diaries and journals—museums in miniature—illuminated by exquisite watercolors and strong sketches."

"Lilias's paintings, which Ruskin so proudly championed [her early works, before Algeria], are buried in the Print Room of the Ashmolean Museum in Oxford."

Both quotes from Miriam Rockness's "Almost Famous," pp. 23, 24.

One of her major creative and writing efforts might seem obvious to us now, but she was among those at the forefront of her missions era with the idea to create and publish booklets that would look and feel Arab to an Arab reader. The written word had one advantage over the spoken word; if a person would take reading material home, he could read and re-read it in the privacy of his home without having to make objections for the sake of appearances.

Lilias and her co-workers wrote many stories and parables that displayed various aspects of Jesus and the gospel. She illustrated the stories and made elaborate Arab-style borders for the covers and pages.

> First, at a time when most literature for Moslems was dealing
> . . . with the great points of difficulty and difference between
> the two religions, Miss Trotter wrote stories that, with all their
> intimate knowledge of Moslem ways and thoughts, appealed
> first to the fundamental *likenesses*, the great human needs of
> all souls. And secondly . . . Miss Trotter gave to all her leaflets
> a touch of colour and of Oriental beauty, with two-colour
> designs or little pictures that looked artistically *right* with the
> Arabic script instead of foreign and strange.[103]

Her outlook was not limited to the Muslims of Algeria. Excellent Arabic literature could be used across the whole Arab world. To a Middle Easterner, even today, the visible beauty of a piece of literature in some way validates its worth.

## ANNIVERSARY OPPOSITION

For many years, March seemed to bring again the greatest depths of difficulty, whether physical, spiritual, or political. Lilias thought it was Satan's recognition of the anniversary of their arrival in his territory.

The month of March in 1918 brought a staggering change to her life.

> The entry on the last page of the Financial Report—
> "Examined and found correct, February 5th, 1918"—stands
> out with a meaning, little thought of when it went to the
> printer a few days later, for the balance sheet, with the "make-

---

[103] Constance Padwick, quoted in Pigott, p. 244.

up" of its preceding pages, was the last bit of Algerian Mission Band service that Blanche Haworth rendered. By the time the proof came back, she was unconscious with fever, and on March 9th, *the anniversary that closed the thirty years* of night toil in this land, she passed, all unknowing that she was going, to the shore where the Master stood waiting.[104]

Blanche Haworth had left England with Lilias in 1888, and they had ministered together all these thirty years. Her death meant the end of the deep friendship with the person who knew Lilias best in all the world.

Together they had founded the Algiers Mission Band. Lilias lived another ten years and saw the AMB grow to include twenty-nine workers with outposts in at least fourteen desert towns. The AMB merged in 1964 with North Africa Mission, which changed its name to Arab World Ministries in 1987.

It's hard to imagine how Lilias and Blanche and their co-workers—mainly single women—accomplished all they did, considering the health and climate and spiritual challenges. They developed ways for Arab believers to become financially independent. They offered a "family camp" setting, where groups could hear the gospel away from the normal cultural pressures. And they acted as matchmakers—filling in for the natural family—for Arab Christians wishing to marry.

And always they were trying to draw others into their call and vision. It is possible that they were the first to create a short-term mission plan. There were opportunities to represent the Muslim cause to the international Christian church through speaking in churches and at international conferences.

## THE LAST YEARS

During the final three years of her life, Lilias's failing heart confined her to her room. She shifted the responsibilities of leadership of the Algerian Mission Band to others. She said, "Long ago, in the past, it was a joy to think that God needed one. Now it is a far deeper joy to feel and see that He does not need one, that He has it all in hand."[105]

With her last strength, she finished *The Way of the Sevenfold Secret,*

---

[104] Ibid., p. 173 (emphasis added).
[105] Ibid., p. 226.

a book to show Jesus to the desert mystics—the Sufis— with whom she had interacted during her desert treks.

At one point in her life, someone described her:

> "She was still and created a stillness," as some one wrote after seeing her for the first time. "It was lovely seeing Miss Trotter; she is beautiful to feel near. I love the quiet of her." This was many years after, when the fight had been long and hard. It was the stillness of strength, the white heat of iron from the furnace.[106]

This stillness often would have been her daytime aspect, especially after she was restricted to her bed. But when she was alone, especially at night, she was a warrior.

> The map of Algeria and Tunisia—her "manual of intercession"— hung over her bed, and she would strategize and agonize in prayer under it, with lamp lit until the early hours of the morning, "of such intercession as only lovers make." Inscribed on the map in her own calligraphy was the rally, "Take heed to the ministry which thou hast received in the Lord that thou fulfill it."[107]

She realized that prayer is not necessarily strengthened by being physically present in the place one is praying about. On the contrary, perhaps one prays more intently far away.

> The powerlessness to go gives an intensity to the joy of it. One can stand in spirit among the dear mud-houses of Tolga, and the domed roofs of Souf, and the horseshoe arches of Tozeur, and the tiled huts buried in prickly-pear hedges in the hills, and *bring down* the working of the Holy Ghost, "By faith in that Name," perhaps more effectively than if one were bodily there. One can shut the door, as it were, and stand alone with God as one cannot on the spot, with the thronging outward distractions of the visible.[108]

---

[106] Ibid., pp. 13-14.

[107] Lisa M. Sinclair, "The Legacy of Isabella Lilias Trotter," *International Bulletin of Missionary Research*, January 2001, p. 33. Quotations are taken from an early biography, Constance E. Padwick, *I. Lilias Trotter of Algiers* (Croydon: Watson, n.d.).

[108] Pigott, pp. 103-104.

One of her friends described the change in Lilias as she moved closer to death, the gate of heaven.

> [I remember] a meditation of Lilias Trotter's on the "glorious body" of the Resurrection. "Suppose," she mused, "that instead of blood every vein were to be filled with *light!*" Almost it seemed in the last year of her life as though this were happening in herself, so strangely beautiful was the shining of spiritual light in a frail and outwearied body.

> On August 27, 1928, her friends sang "Jesus, Lover of my Soul." Lilias looked out the window and exclaimed, "A chariot and six horses!"

> A friend asked, "You are seeing beautiful things?"
> "Yes, many beautiful things."
> She lifted her hands in prayer, and almost immediately, calmly drew her last breath.[109]

Lilias Trotter did not see the answer to her prayer for a multitude of Muslims to turn to Christ. Then, as now, the ground is hard. Scattered through Lilias Trotter's writings are parables of yearning for that glorious blossom of God's spring coming into the Muslim world.

> God has left, as yet, one bit of his spiritual orchard with leaf-less boughs, while the tracery of fresh green is seen far and wide—it may well be that he needs no slow preparatory stages of evident advance towards the goal. A week ago, up here in the hills, they said one day, "A cherry tree is in bloom." The day after, whole orchards were snow-white. Who can tell which tiny movement is the precursor of blossom-time in the bare trees of Islam? . . . And the marvel of springtime in the Muslim world will stand revealed, through "the unknown reserves of the Divine resources."[110]

Lilias Trotter's letters, journal entries, reports, and devotionals reflect a steady, strong, serene tone. Sometimes there is discouragement

---

[109] Recounted in Rockness, *A Passion for the Impossible*, p. 273.
[110] Padwick, *I. Lilias Trotter of Algiers*, p. 18.

or yearning. But in one entry, anger leaps from the page. She was on a ship crossing the Mediterranean, returning home to Algiers after a conference in Europe.

> One who is traveling with us was talking of the way in which, in the Church's outlook on the mission field, the view is still very general that the Moslems are a doomed race.
>
> A *doomed* race!! It does not sound very like "The *God of Hope*," or "the *God of Love*." A doomed creed is nearer the mark; the husk that imprisons the seed is doomed, that is all. Hallelujah![111]

God had given Lilias the threefold prayer as they entered Algeria, and it was the core of her prayers after that—open doors, open hearts, and open heavens. In 1923, after thirty-five years, she wrote about God's answers to that prayer. It stands as a benediction on his work in Algeria and remains a petition to be prayed by all who care about Algeria and the broader Arab world.

> The threefold prayer of early days comes back to memory. First, that doors might be opened: that is answered already above all we could ask or think. Then, that hearts might be opened: and that is coming—the attitude has swept round from apathy to hostility, and from hostility to a large measure of welcome. Next, and last, that the heavens may be opened— when that is granted, the harvest will come.[112]

It is an odd thing, from our perspective, that God should prepare Lilias for missions as he did. She suffered permanent heart damage when she was twenty-nine. She shared responsibility for the care of her invalid sister. And by the time she even thought of missions as a possibility she was "too old." This causes me to ask myself some questions. I hope you also will ask them prayerfully of yourself.

---

[111] Pigott, p. 149.
[112] Ibid., p. 195.

- Who ought to be involved in ministry, perhaps even missions?
- What are true hindrances to following a call to some sort of ministry?
- What are the required qualifications for following God's call?
- What preparation does it take?

Is it impossible that I, or my daughter, or my granddaughter should do such a thing? Maybe. Maybe not. It doesn't depend on me. Who is my God? Is he not the same God who called Lilias Trotter, prepared her, moved her, and sustained her in Algeria for forty years? Is he not the same yesterday and today and forever?

But how can I know what lies in the future? How will I know how to get ready? I can't really know. Lilias must have been mulling such thoughts when she wrote:

> How many of us have said and sung with all our hearts "Anywhere with Jesus," but at the same time we did not realize all that it meant for us. Indeed at home, and surrounded by all that home means, we could not know. When the test comes we must not forget that "anywhere" means for missionaries something different from life in England, and let us take very good care not to make a misery of anything that "anywhere" brings us.
>
> To us in Algeria it must mean sometime or other, Arab food. Do we object to it? And mice, do we mind them? And mosquitoes, do we think them dreadful? In some parts it means close contact with dirt and repulsive disease. Yet if Jesus is there, what have we possibly to complain of? It means living among a stiff-necked and untrue people and struggling with a strange and difficult language. And yet let us evermore write over all our miseries, big, and for the most part very little, these transforming words "With Jesus." And then the very breath of Heaven will breathe upon our whole being and we shall be glad.[113]

Perhaps God's call to me right now is that I be right here. But I don't assume it will always be so. In the meantime, I want to be like Adeline Braithwaite and Lelie Duff, Lilias's two friends whose earnest prayers

---

[113] Rockness, *A Passion for the Impossible*, p. 202.

and glowing spirits inspired Lilias to ask God to give her what they had. What he gave her was a fellowship with him that led her to Algeria.

Adeline and Lelie are examples—like Sarah Edwards exhorting Samuel Hopkins—of women who spoke and prayed faithfully, without fully realizing the ongoing impact God would make through them. Adeline and Lelie were responsible, in part, for forty years of faithful ministry in Algeria, though they themselves never went. Lilias expressed her gratitude:

> Through Eternity I shall thank God for the silent flame in the hearts of those two friends and what they did for me. Neither of them has ever had their path opened into foreign work, but the light of the Day that is coming will show what He has let them do in kindling others.[114]

Lilias Trotter, by human standards, should have been a famous, but frail, artist. She was certainly not healthy enough to be a missionary in such a demanding climate and culture as Algeria. And yet, as she affirmed, her God is the God of the impossible.

*There is a woman, special to me, who was in my mind as I read about Lilias Trotter and Algeria. Barbara was my almost-relative—the sister of the husband of the sister of my husband—and became my friend in a time of great grief. She spent her adult life with North Africa Mission, serving in Algeria for as long as she could, and then with Arabs in France until she died. Physical life was easier for Barbara in the 1960s and 1970s than it was for Lilias Trotter at the turn of the last century. But the hearts of the people were not so different. And so this story of Lilias Trotter of Algeria is dedicated to Barbara Bowers.*

---

[114] Pigott, p. 84.

*F*or the foolishness of God is wiser than men,
and the weakness of God is stronger than men.
For consider your calling, brothers:
not many of you were wise according to worldly standards,
not many were powerful, not many were of noble birth.
But God chose what is foolish in the world to shame the wise;
God chose what is weak in the world to shame the strong;
God chose what is low and despised in the world,
even things that are not, to bring to nothing things that are,
so that no human being might boast in the presence of God.
He is the source of your life in Christ Jesus,
whom God made our wisdom and our righteousness and
    sanctification and redemption.
Therefore, as it is written, "Let the one who boasts,
boast in the Lord."

1 CORINTHIANS 1:25-31

*I* can do all things through him who strengthens me.

PHILIPPIANS 4:13

# GLADYS AYLWARD
*Faithful in Humility*

⟨∞⟩

In China, the nineteenth century ended with a bloody rampage against foreigners and Chinese people who associated with them. Thousands of Chinese Christians and more than 230 foreigners, many of them missionaries, were slain by members of a revolutionary society called the Fists of Righteous Harmony, nicknamed "Boxers." Their war cry was, "Exterminate foreigners, kill devils!"[115] September 1901 marked the end of the Boxer Rebellion.

Five months later, on February 24, 1902, on the other side of the globe, a baby girl was born in Edmonton, an area of North London. Mr. and Mrs. Thomas Aylward named their first child Gladys May. Neither the Aylwards nor most of their working-class neighbors would ever move far from where they themselves had been born. They certainly never dreamed that Gladys would someday live in China's Shanxi Province, which had been a hotbed of Boxer brutality.

Thomas Aylward was a postman and vicar's warden at St. Aldhelm's Church. Mrs. Aylward was a homemaker who spoke sometimes at the mission hall against the evils of drink. Gladys's parents took her regularly to church services and to Sunday school.

Gladys was not a good student, and she didn't like school; so she dropped out at fourteen, not really qualified for any job. Her parents helped her find a place in a Penny Bazaar—the "dollar store" of that day. Then she went to work in a grocery store. After that she went into service, working as a nanny and then a parlor maid in wealthy households. These jobs didn't pay well, but Gladys was enjoying life in the city. In the evenings she attended drama classes, because what she

---

[115] The account of Fei Ch'i-hao, a Christian man in the town of Fen Chou Fu, can be read at http://www.fordham.edu/halsall/mod/1900Fei-boxers.html (accessed 2-16-05). The account online is by Luella Miner, *Two Heroes of Cathay* (N.Y.: Fleming H. Revell, 1907), pp. 63-128, quoted in Eva Jane Price, *China Journal, 1889-1900* (N.Y.: Charles Scribner's Sons, 1989), pp. 245-247, 254-261, 268-274.

really wanted to be was an actress. By now she had become impatient with religious things.

## WHY NOT YOU?

But God was getting her ready for something else. In her autobiography she wrote:

> One night, for some reason I can never explain, I went to a religious meeting. There, for the first time, I realized that God had a claim on my life, and I accepted Jesus Christ as my Saviour. I joined the Young Life Campaign, and in one of their magazines I read an article about China that made a terrific impression on me. To realize that millions of Chinese had never heard of Jesus Christ was to me a staggering thought, and I felt we ought to do something about it.[116]

The main point of the article was that for the first time a pilot had flown from Shanghai to Lanchow, far inland. Gladys probably had never heard of Lanchow and had no idea that someday she would visit there and live nearby. Not realizing yet that this article was meant for *her*, she tried to get her Christian friends interested in taking the gospel to China. But no one cared. She approached her brother, thinking he would surely go if she promised to help him.

> "Not me!" he said bluntly. "That's an old maid's job. Why don't you go yourself?"
> "Old maid's job indeed!" I thought angrily. But the thrust had gone home. Why should I try pushing other people off to China? Why didn't I go myself?[117]

She wasn't a nurse or a teacher, so she wasn't sure whether there was a place for her on the mission field. But she knew she could talk. Maybe God could use that. So she applied to the China Inland Mission.[118] On December 12, 1929, their Candidates' Committee took note of her conversion to Christianity and her "manifest strength of

---

[116] Gladys Aylward and Christine Hunter, *The Little Woman* (Chicago: Moody Press, 1999), pp. 7-8.
[117] Ibid., p. 8.
[118] China Inland Mission (now OMF International—Overseas Missionary Fellowship) was founded by Hudson Taylor in 1865.

character." Although there is no direct mention of her inadequate schooling and mediocre educational skills, those limitations are implied in the conditional recommendation of "one term's testing to see if she is able to settle down to regular study."[119]

At the Women's Training Home, it was a new experience for Gladys to be "above stairs" with the other trainees, rather than being "below stairs" with the house servants. The three-month term was filled with classroom work, Bible study, personal devotions, Sunday school teaching in rough neighborhoods, and hearing reports about China and the difficulties of getting there and living there. Gladys did well in the practical, active settings, but she couldn't seem to understand and learn from the lectures and books.

At the end of the time, the committee judged that she was not qualified and that her educational background was too limited. They were also concerned that the Chinese language would be too difficult for her, especially at her age—her late twenties. Gladys was stunned. She had been so sure that God wanted her to go to China.

## PERSONALIZED MISSIONS TRAINING

And he did. But he planned to send her in a different way, a way that would fit her. Before he sent her, God put her through her own personal missionary candidate school and an apprenticeship that he'd planned specifically for her. Some of the subjects were similar to what she'd have received at candidate school, but the classroom was life itself.

Perhaps her first lessons were in the area of prayer, even while she was still struggling through CIM's Candidate Training. At the end of her time there, she said to the committee, "I'm sorry I haven't been able to learn much at the college, but I have learned to pray, really pray as I never did before, and that is something for which I'll always be grateful."[120]

When the missions committee asked Gladys not to return for further training, she wondered if God had closed her way to China. Especially when one of the concerned mission executives asked about her plans and offered her a job in Bristol helping Dr. and Mrs. Fisher,

---

[119] Phyllis Thompson, *A Transparent Woman* (Grand Rapids, Mich.: Zondervan Publishing House, 1971), p. 18.
[120] Aylward and Hunter, p. 9.

who had recently retired from China. She accepted because the door to the future she had planned was shut now. But going to work for the Fishers felt like a step backward. It put her back in household service, not what she dreamed of. But in this setting, God was placing her with older, wiser spiritual mentors. She said later,

> I learned many lessons from them; their implicit faith in God was a revelation to me. Never before had I met anyone who trusted him so utterly, so implicitly and so obediently. They knew God as their friend, not as a being far away, and they lived with him every day.
>
> Dr. and Mrs. Fisher told me stories of their own lives overseas. "God never lets you down. He sends you, guides you and provides for you. Maybe He doesn't answer your prayers as you want them answered, but he does answer them."

The real question for Gladys was this: Was *no* from China Inland Mission the same as *no* from God? Or was it simply God's way of leaving her open to a new plan?

> "How am I to know if he wants me to go to China or to stay in Bristol?" I queried.
>
> "He will show you in his own good time. Keep on watching and praying."[121]

That may not seem like very significant advice, but it was what she needed—the exhortation to keep on watching and praying.

If her ability to talk was going to be her main asset on a challenging mission field, she would need ministry experience. Even before she had applied to CIM, God had been giving her opportunities for evangelism. The minutes of the CIM Candidates' Committee notes that "she has borne a consistent witness in her place of employment and has worked in the open air and at young people's meetings."[122]

Later, when she left the Fischers, she moved to Wales to work as a rescue sister in Swansea, a port town. Every night she was down at the docks, trying to persuade women to go home or to go with her to

---

121 Ibid.
122 Thompson, p. 18.

the rescue mission. In rough waterside pubs, she'd face down drunken sailors, if that's what it took, to rescue the young girls with them. Then she'd take the girls back to the mission hostel.

## A HOUSE SERVANT WHO WAS CALLED

This kind of challenging ministry helped her realize she would need to know the Bible more thoroughly if God ever did take her to China. So she began reading at the first page. Her style of living and speaking was straightforward, and that's the way she understood what she read. When she learned about God guiding Abraham to a strange place and about Moses defying difficult people to follow God, she thought, *If I were to go to China I would have to be willing to move and give up what little comfort and security I had.*[123] So she didn't wait. She left Swansea and moved back to London to work and save money for the fare to China.

Still perplexed about God's call in her life, her Bible reading brought her to the story of Nehemiah. His story was of special interest to Gladys, the parlor maid, because Nehemiah was in service too, as a sort of butler. He had to obey his employer, just as Gladys did. But that didn't stop Nehemiah from going where God sent him.

Almost like a voice in the room she heard, "Gladys Aylward, is Nehemiah's God your God?"

"Yes, of course."
"Then do what Nehemiah did, and go."
"But I am not Nehemiah."
"No, but I am his God."
"That settled it," she said later. "I believed those were my marching orders."[124]

Later at another crucial moment in her life, deep in the interior of China, God would use similar words to assure Gladys of his eternal power. That next time, his words would be given to her by a child when she'd lost sight of God's presence.

It was invigorating to have marching orders. But traveling to China was expensive. Gladys continued to try to think of a way to get there,

---

123 Aylward and Hunter, p. 11.
124 Ibid., pp. 11-12.

but discouragement was setting in. She wouldn't have the endorsement or recommendation of a mission board, so if she were going, it would have to be on her own initiative and probably with her own money. Since Gladys Aylward didn't know for sure she was going to China or where in the country she would be or what she would be doing there, much less how she was going to pay for it, she was keenly aware that her provision was totally from God. If God was calling her, he would provide for her.

It's ironic to realize that her new parlor maid position was in the home of Sir Francis Younghusband, a legendary adventurer who had explored remote areas of China and Tibet. It's doubtful that he even noticed that there was a new house servant. And neither he nor Gladys would have imagined that a parlor maid would undertake adventures in China that would rival his.

## CONFIRMATION

When she arrived at the Younghusband home, she went up to her room to settle in. Unpacking, she spread out on the bed her total assets. They added up to one Bible, one copy of *Daily Light*,[125] and three coins that amounted to twopence halfpenny, which was all her money and was just as meager an amount as it sounds. "O God," she prayed, "here's everything I have. If you want me, I am going to China with these."[126] As if in answer to that prayer, her mistress called her downstairs. She wanted to repay the fare Gladys had paid to get there. Gladys returned to her room clutching three shillings. In one moment, through no effort of her own, God had increased her savings more than a thousand percent.[127]

This seemed to Gladys like God's promise that he would provide her fare to China. So at the first opportunity she went to the travel agency to start making payments on her passage to sail to China. The booking agent was incredulous. Such a woman would never be able to

---

[125] *Daily Light on the Daily Path: A Devotional Textbook for Every Day of the Year, in the Very Words of Scripture*, Jonathan Bagster, ed., first published in New York by the American Tract Society, ca. 1875. The original text of this classic devotional book is online at http://www.mun.ca/rels/restmov/texts/dasc/DLDP0000.HTM (accessed 2-16-05). Each devotional uses Scripture to meditate on Scripture. A newer version using the *English Standard Version* is also now available (Wheaton, Ill.: Crossway Books, 2002). For more than 100 years, *Daily Light* is mentioned in the stories of many missionaries on every inhabited continent.

[126] Aylward and Hunter, p. 12.

[127] The United Kingdom adopted its decimal currency system in 1971. Gladys's coins were from the old system. One shilling equaled twelve old pennies.

afford the ninety-pound ship fare. He thought she was crazy. Somehow he let it slip that the rail journey across Europe and Siberia and into China cost about half as much. Well, of course, Gladys knew right away she would travel by train. She refused to hear his arguments that it was impossible because of war between Russia and China. Her persistent "deafness" won out, and he reluctantly agreed to accept regular deposits until the full amount was in.

The primary way God provided her fare was through Gladys's own hard work. After her long days as a parlor maid, she took extra work in the evenings helping to serve at parties or whatever she could find to do. She saved everything she earned, eking from every worn article of clothing just one more wearing and then one more again.

God provided necessities in unexpected ways through the generosity of others. One day Gladys's mistress had been planning to attend a garden party with a friend, but the friend became ill. So she invited Gladys to accompany her. Gladys was thrilled, but had no appropriate clothes for such an event. The lady lent Gladys some of her own. Afterward, when Gladys tried to return them, her employer asked her to keep them. These were of much better quality than anything Gladys would ever have gotten for herself, and they served her well for a long time.

Another unexpected providence was that, bit by bit, Gladys deposited the full amount of her fare in less than a year, though she had expected it to take fully three years. This meant she would arrive in China when she was still thirty, instead of thirty-two. At the time, this seemed important to her. God had given her two bonus years.

## A TRANSPARENT WOMAN

What kind of person was this missionary candidate who had gone through God's personalized candidate school? What were the ingredients that mixed together to make Gladys Aylward? She was not a student of books, but she studied people. She knew the needs of the poor people in Swansea and often gave them her own clothes. At the other end of the spectrum, she observed the family and guests in the fine houses where she worked, learning how they spoke and what they spoke about.

Still, she remained a straightforward, unsubtle, simple person. Phyllis Thompson wrote that her demeanor did not shape itself to make an impression or to try to be accepted or to gain friends. Thompson said that later in her life, in China, Gladys "smiled when there was something to smile about, glared when she was moved to indignation, frowned when she was puzzled (which occurred often in connection with the ramifications of arithmetic) and laughed like a child when she was happy. She was, in fact, as transparent as water."[128]

And yet her bluntness must have been flavored with winsomeness. What lady in those days would ever have taken a maid along as a peer—not as a servant—to a gathering of her own set? And yet, there was something about Gladys that led her mistress, in spite of the strong strata of society at that time in England, to take her as a guest to a society garden party.

Gladys was simple and straightforward, with the bravado to walk the midnight Swansea streets, risking meeting up with intoxicated men who might mistake her for a prostitute. On the other hand, she was reticent to talk about herself. Much later, in 1949, when Alan Burgess was trying to write the story of her life, she didn't want to be interviewed. She said nothing worth writing about had ever happened to her. He half believed her. A missionary going to tell people about God—what kind of story is that? That's exactly what missionaries are supposed to do. He persisted for months and heard only story after story about preaching and villages, just about what he expected. Then one day she casually mentioned a delay caused by trouble at the prison. Prison! That was something out of the ordinary. Sentence by sentence, event by event, Burgess dragged from her the story of Gladys Aylward single-handedly stopping a prison riot.

But not really single-handedly. She would have told anyone that everything she did was "through him who strengthens me" (Philippians 4:13). After explaining how Gladys Aylward was as transparent as water, Phyllis Thompson (whose biography of Gladys Aylward is entitled The Transparent Woman) describes her theology.

Her theology was the same, clear and uncomplicated. There was a living God, and she was His servant. There was a loathsome Creature called Satan, and she was his enemy. There was an immortal soul in every human being proceeding to an eter-

128 Thompson, p. 117.

nity in either Heaven or Hell. Her job in life was to convince people that if they would but put their trust in Jesus Christ her Lord, who had died on the cross for them, they would get straight on the road to Heaven. And since Jesus Christ had come to life again, and had promised to be with those who trusted and obeyed Him, however beset with trials and temptations the road to Heaven might prove to be, they need fear nothing, for He would never let them down.[129]

She was a dark-haired, shrill-voiced Cockney, only four feet, ten inches tall. And yet she was going to make a large, deep impact in the Shanxi Province of China.

## Family and Friends

Her parents must have been bemused by their parlor maid daughter's steady progress toward the unthinkable. Soon after Gladys began to look toward China and could talk of little else, her father apparently had heard enough one day. He snapped, "Go on with you! Talk about going to China—talk, talk! That's all you can do—just talk!"[130] Gladys took up that gauntlet and began to make real steps toward China. Perhaps it hadn't occurred to him yet that something might come of all that talk.

Gladys's mother was responsible indirectly for finding Gladys a place in China. When Gladys felt sure God was calling her to China, the question remained: Where? Where would she go when she arrived in the country? China's a huge place. Whom was she going to meet? Was there anyone there to work with, anyone to help her get started? To solve those problems, God took Gladys back to her parents' house. Gladys had contracted pneumonia from her nights as a rescue sister out on the docks in the damp, cold air. So she went home to recuperate.

Sometime during those days, Gladys went with her mother to a Primitive Methodist meeting to pray for strength and healing. At that gathering, she heard about Jeannie Lawson—an elderly Scottish widow in China who had been praying for a young woman to come and assist her. One biographer writes:

---

[129] Ibid.
[130] Ibid., p. 16.

God had kept her from feeling well so that she would go to the meeting that night to pray for her health. God wanted her to hear of Mrs. Lawson. She had been right all the time. The Lord did want her to go to China and everything that had happened to her had been leading her to this meeting at the Wood Green Church.[131]

God used the next three years to change Mr. and Mrs. Aylward's assumptions about what a girl from their neighborhood might do and how far she might go. Gladys found her family and friends to be strong supporters of her call. When Gladys's fare was collected and she was ready to travel, she says, "My father insisted that I go home for a few days, and all of them did their best for me. Ivy Benson, a friend who also was a maid, gave me a badly needed suitcase, though it wasn't until long after that I discovered the anonymous gift came from her. My mother sewed secret pockets into my coat and in an old corselet [undergarment] for my tickets, passport, Bible, fountain pen, and two travelers' checks worth one pound each. Another friend gave me an old fur coat and, between them, the family fitted me out with warm clothes."[132]

In those meager gifts, we see family and friends wrapping her around with every physical comfort they could give her. They were far from rich, so it wasn't much, but it was everything they could give. Each item was a token of their love for her—all they could give. And those gifts were more than tokens. They were necessities. In fact, the fur coat was going to save her life in just a few weeks. She wrote later, full of gratitude:

> How good they were to me. I realize more fully now as I look back. How great was the sacrifice my parents were making in allowing their daughter to go off alone to a place thousands of miles away, knowing full well that in all probability they would never see her again. How much I have to thank them for, that they did not try to hold me back.[133]

Actually they *would* see her again, but not for seventeen years. Other missionaries at that time had furloughs, though not as frequently

[131] Catherine Swift, *Gladys Aylward* (Minneapolis: Bethany House Publishers, 1989), pp. 13-14.
[132] Aylward and Hunter, p.15.
[133] Ibid.

as is usual now. But Gladys went, expecting never to return to England. She had just enough money to get there, nothing more. If God was calling her to China, she was going without thought of return. She was already seeing China as her permanent home.

## INTO THE UNKNOWN

On October 15, 1932, Gladys set out from London. Her suitcase was filled with all the food for her journey, because she had no money to buy meals along the way. Dangling from her suitcase were a bedroll, a teakettle, a saucepan, a small camping-type stove, and an army blanket bundled around a few clothes. This tiny, simple, unpolished woman had never traveled outside her own country and language. Now she was setting out alone into a new world and life, able only to guess what lay ahead. But she knew that God had been preparing her for this and that he was going with her and ahead of her.

Between London and The Hague, a Dutch couple on the train heard she was going to China as a missionary. They bought her hot chocolate and cookies, a sweet blessing to a woman with no money. Then they promised to pray for her every night at 9:00 as long as they lived, and later to meet her in heaven. This was sweeter and richer than any chocolate. It was like the last touch of the outstretched fingers of home, bidding farewell and calling, "I love you." When the train reached The Hague, the couple left her with a blessing and an English pound note. This pound note would later save her life.

All along the way Gladys could see God protecting her and providing for her. In Berlin a girl with a little English helped her through customs and gave her a bed for the night at her home. Traveling toward Moscow, a Polish man who couldn't understand English gave her an apple and a stamp and posted a letter for her.

Ten days into her trip, a man with a little English was traveling some distance through Russia in the train. He served as a providential messenger from God when he warned her that no trains were going to Harbin, where she had expected to change trains. With the warning, she was able to watch for an alternate route as she traveled.

Past Chita, far north in Russia, the train stopped at the edge of a war zone. The train was going no further. There was nowhere for Gladys to go except to return where she'd come from, and no way to go but on foot, lugging her awkward baggage bundle through the bitter cold and deep snow. Finally, when she was exhausted, she lay down to sleep on top of her suitcase. Her "new" fur coat, the gift of a friend, was her blanket. She was surprised to hear what she thought were dogs barking and howling nearby. Years later when she realized they were actually wolves, she recognized that part of God's kind provision that night had been ignorance—what she didn't know had let her sleep in peace. That she woke up the next morning was another gift. According to laws of nature, she probably should have died of cold and exposure while sleeping outside in the bitter Russian winter.

After another long day of trekking, she reached Chita, which she had left several days before. She was arrested immediately upon her arrival. "Your visa said you left Chita. Why are you here?" the local officials demanded. She wasn't able to speak Russian to explain. In the confusion, a photo fell from her Bible. It was a portrait of her brother in his uniform, the uniform of a musician in the band of the British army. To Gladys's interrogators, he appeared to be a very important person. Apparently they didn't want to risk offending such a man, so they gave Gladys a new visa and ticket and sent her on her way.

At the next railway stop, God provided English again when she needed it. She didn't know where to go, and she didn't know how to find out. Through a train window she spotted a person who didn't look Russian. She called out, "How shall I get to Harbin?" The passing stranger had this piece of God's itinerary for her in English: "Go to Vladivostok."

In Vladivostok, the hotel clerk took her passport. He didn't return it, but put it away, talking as if she were staying in Russia. As Gladys moved away from the desk, a girl she had never before seen walked along beside her and spoke in her ear. She warned Gladys to get away right away. "Get your passport back. Tonight an old man will knock at your door. Go with him."

Who was this girl? Could Gladys trust her? Yes, she should probably leave Vladivostok as soon as possible, but was it wise to leave at night with a strange man? And besides, how could she retrieve her passport from the "safekeeping" of the hotel staff?

That night the hotel clerk came to her door and began to dangle her passport just out of her reach, tantalizing her. She lunged forward and was able to grab it. Then he started into the room, growling, "You can't stop me." It wasn't clear what he most wanted, Gladys or her passport. Gladys stood her ground. "God is here. Touch me, and you will see. He has put a barrier between you and me. Go!" The man went.

Later that night the old man knocked on her door, and she followed him. He led her to the girl who had warned her earlier in the day. The girl took her to a Japanese ship. Gladys had no money, but if God wanted her to escape on this ship, he would provide the way. In the end, she did somehow persuade the ship's officers to accept her as a passenger.

As she fled to the ship, some Russians caught up with her and physically tried to restrain her from boarding. In the midst of the scuffle, she remembered the pound note the Dutch friends had given her on the train. She managed to pull it out and she waved it in front of them. While her pursuers scrambled for the money, she ran onto the ship. God had used British currency—which should have been no good outside of England—to save her.

Gladys Aylward had never heard the phrase "culture shock" because it hadn't been invented yet. But she knew its reality. Missionary candidates nowadays go through training to help them prepare for their new life in an unfamiliar setting. Gladys wasn't offered that opportunity by a mission board, but God seems to have used her trans-Siberian travel as her own private boot camp.

Gladys was indeed shocked by what she saw in Russia—by the conditions of the people and by the way she herself was treated. After her midnight escape from Vladivostok, she discovered that her passport had been altered by someone in Russia. Where her visa listed her occupation as "missionary," the word had been changed to "machinist." Machinists were desperately needed in Russia, and the regime was not hesitant to abduct people who could be useful for its purposes. Someone had made a serious effort to keep her in Russia. If that had happened, she would never have been heard from again.

Safe on the Japanese ship, a small everyday occurrence may have given Gladys second thoughts about her future life. Rice was the large part of every meal in a Japanese diet, just as it would be in most of China. But Gladys found rice very hard to swallow. What would this mean for her? She didn't know yet that God was saving up a small, sweet providence for her. He was leading her to Shanxi Province where the staple is not rice, but millet and noodles.

## AT LAST—CHINA

The ship docked in Japan, and after a few days Gladys sailed from Kobe to Tientsin (now Tienjin). Gladys Aylward, former parlor maid, finally was standing on Chinese soil!

We don't know precisely what she felt, but one thing we know. She looked around and realized that God had been preparing her for this day since before her birth. Many years later, Gladys told Elisabeth Elliot about two childhood heartaches. One had been that all the other girls had golden curls while she had black hair. The other was that everybody else kept growing while she stopped at four feet, ten inches. Now in Tientsin, she stood in the midst of the people God had prepared her for. They all had black hair, and none of them had kept growing.[134]

Mrs. Jeannie Lawson had sent Mr. Lu to Tientsin to meet Gladys and accompany her to Yangcheng. She still had ten days of traveling ahead of her before she reached her new home. Through Peking (Beijing), over the country by train, bus, and mule litter, across three mountain ranges and numerous rivers they traveled. In some towns there were mission outposts where they could stop for rest and refreshment. In Tsechow, the last town before Yangcheng, Mrs. Smith provided her with the quilted trousers and jackets of the country women. "We missionaries all wear Chinese clothes," Mrs. Smith said. "We want to be as like the Chinese as possible—and their clothes are much more sensible than ours, anyway!"[135] So Gladys was able finally to change out of the orange dress she had worn since she left England five and a half weeks before. Gladys wrote, "How much I had seen! How much I had learned in those weeks! And above all, for how much I had to worship my God!"

In Yangcheng, Gladys finally met Mrs. Jeannie Lawson. Mrs. Lawson had spent most of her life in China, first with her husband, then as a widow. Recently she had bought a dilapidated roadside inn. Her dream was that the Inn of the Eight Happinesses would become a regular overnight stopping place for muleteers who passed through Yangcheng on the road—the only road—from Hopeh to Honan. Each evening when the muleteers had been fed and were resting, she would tell them stories from the Bible.

---

[134] Recounted by Elisabeth Elliot on "Gateway to Joy," broadcast July 22, 1999. She told Gladys Aylward's story July 19-30, 1999, http://www.backtothebible.org/gateway/today/1697 (accessed 3/23/05).
[135] Thompson, p. 39.

## CALLED TO MULES?

The Boxer Rebellion was thirty years in the past, but rural China was still suspicious of outside influences. It was going to be a challenge to get mule drivers to stay in a place run by "foreign devils." This became Gladys's first missionary assignment—persuading the muleteers to stop at the Inn of the Eight Happinesses. Each evening, she stood outside the gate calling out Chinese words that Mrs. Lawson's cook had taught her, something like a sideshow barker. "We have no bugs. We have no fleas. Good, good, good! Come, come, come!" Then when the mule drivers still wouldn't turn through the inn's gate, Gladys would have to reach out to grab the bridle of the lead mule and drag him in by main force. Wherever the lead mule went, the other mules followed. And where the mules went, the muleteers followed, however unwillingly. Once the mules had crowded into the courtyard, it was too difficult to think of turning that train of stubborn beasts around and moving out again. No one was going anywhere till morning.

Since Jeannie Lawson and the cook could speak Chinese, they were the ones who fed the men and then sat by the fire to tell them stories from the Scripture. That left Gladys out in the cold with the mules. Someone had to scrape off the day's mud and feed the animals. This provided an unexpected incentive for learning Chinese, the language that was supposed to be too difficult for her. When she wasn't tending mules, she spent time in the village, listening and trying to speak. She wrote, "The language is very difficult, but I am a good mimic and so am picking up little bits without study."[136]

By the end of only a year, Gladys could make herself understood in Chinese, and her repertoire of stories was growing. So it might seem easy for someone to point a finger at the mission board who turned her away and to say, "See how wrong you were!" But Gladys herself said much later,

> Looking back I cannot blame them. I know, if no one else does, how stupid I must have seemed then. The fact that I learned not only to speak, but also to read and write the Chinese language like a native in later years, is to me one of God's great miracles.[137]

---

[136] Thompson, p. 42.
[137] Aylward and Hunter, p. 8.

Jeannie and Gladys had a short, but stormy relationship. They had little in common except their love of God and the knowledge that they were supposed to be in China. Yet when Mrs. Lawson lay dying, after only a year together, Gladys nursed her, and Mrs. Lawson passed her mantle to Gladys. "God called you to my side, Gladys, in answer to my prayers. He wants you to carry on my work. He will provide. He will bless and protect."[138]

Indeed, God already had blessed and provided. He had provided Mrs. Lawson, who was the reason Gladys traveled to China. He had provided enough overlap time—apprenticeship time—with Mrs. Lawson to prepare Gladys to carry on her work.

Gladys was a young woman by Chinese standards, the only Westerner in that part of China. She spoke Chinese as she had learned it from the muleteers and in the market. She continued at the inn, held services regularly, visited houses, and gave what medical aid she could. As her Chinese improved, she went out to speak in the marketplaces with a Chinese evangelist. During these early months, she stayed close to her new hometown of Yangcheng. But as she felt more at home, God used unexpected means to broaden her field.

## INSPECTING FEET

When Gladys came to China in 1932, the binding of young girls' feet was supposed to be a thing of the past. Foot-binding was the process by which little girls' toes were bent under and wrapped tightly so that the foot was kept as small as possible, maybe only three or four inches long.[139] This was considered attractive and a sign that a family was in

---

[138] Ibid., p. 42.

[139] In 1999, a woman born in 1920, eight years after foot-binding was banned, described what it was like.
Carrying on the custom from the older generations, my feet were bound when I was six years old. Perhaps a six-year-old girl's feet were the perfect length for binding.
My grandmother took about one metre of white cloth which was woven by herself at home and divided it into three long one-metre strips, then the binding started. She left my big toe, and folded down the rest of the toes under the sole of the foot and then used the strips to tie it in many layers.... You can imagine a six-year-old girl's feet and how delicate they were, but if they were tied very tightly and changed the natural shape, how painful it must be. . . . With the pain of the feet, I was forced to push around a big rock used as a mill for grinding. I walked and walked, step by step, many, many circuits in order to form the binding cone shape and to make the process more efficient. The suffering is really beyond people's imagination.
When the feet were unbound, my sisters and I cried, because of the pain which was caused by the unbinding. But when my grandmother rebound our feet, it would be more painful and we cried again.
My sisters and I endured the pain and gradually unbound our feet. We got rid of the long strips first and wore a pair of very tight cloth socks instead. Gradually the feet started to grow again. When I married in 1942, my feet had already become jie fang jiao (liberated feet).

the market for a good husband. When Sun Yat-sen had established the Chinese Republic in 1912, ending the final imperial dynasty in China, one of the earliest actions of the new senate was a ban on foot-binding.

But China is an immense country, a challenging place to enforce new laws, especially for a wobbly new regime. Even more important, a cultural tradition entrenched for a millennium could not be ended easily. Even today, in the first years of the twenty-first century, there are old women in China leaning on sticks or on the arms of family members because their twisted four-inch feet can't support them.

God used feet to open China more widely for Gladys. The government had decreed once again that foot-binding must end and had laid the responsibility on the mandarins, the local representatives of the government. The mandarin approached Gladys and commanded her to find a foot inspector. When she couldn't find one, he appointed her to the position. The mandarin said she would be a good example to the women who had bound feet since she had big feet (size 3!). He would provide a mule for transportation and a couple of soldiers to accompany her.

Gladys saw God's hand in this. After Mrs. Lawson's death, she had been facing difficult questions. How would she support herself? There wasn't enough income from the inn. She thought perhaps God wanted her to spread the gospel further afield, but should she? It wasn't safe to travel far into the mountains. And how would she travel? She wouldn't be able to go far on foot, and she couldn't afford any other transportation.

Now the mandarin was offering her official permission to go anywhere she wished, a steady income, transportation, and protection as she traveled. She wrote later,

> As I look back, I am amazed at the way God opened up the opportunities for service. I had longed to go to China, but never in my wildest dreams had I imagined that God would overrule in such a way that I would be given entrance into

---

I used to watch my feet carefully. They are much smaller than average. I am 1.7 metres tall but my feet are only 22 centimetres long. The big toe seems normal, but the rest of the toes are very flat and folded down under the sole of the foot. There are some small scars between the instep and the toes. The scars were made when my feet were first bound, the bones of the toes were broken and became inflamed, so the scars remained until now. The pain has gone a long time ago.

(The Australian Museum, http://www.austmus.gov.au/bodyart/shaping/Footbinding.htm, accessed 5-6-05.)

every village home [not just every village]; have authority to banish a cruel, horrible custom; have government protection; and be paid to preach the gospel of Jesus Christ as I inspected feet!"[140]

She knew that if she were able to go to the remote villages, she would certainly take the good news of Jesus. So she didn't ask, but told the mandarin she would use the opportunity to preach the gospel. He replied, "From the standpoint of this decree, your teaching is good, because if a woman becomes a Christian she no longer binds her feet."[141]

In later years, she described what those visits were like:

When we came to a village, the soldiers would summon everyone to the village clearing and repeat the Mandarin's instructions about foot-binding. . . .

Then I would start to talk to the people. I would tell them a story. I would get them all laughing and happy and teach them to sing a chorus after I had explained the meaning of the words.

Then I would talk about feet.

"You know that boys' feet and girls' feet are all alike. If God had wanted girls to have little, stunted feet he would have made them like that. And now the government says any who bind their babies' feet will be punished."

It was too late for the older women [if they tried to unbind their feet it would have been excruciatingly painful and they wouldn't have been able to walk at all], but I made the girls unbind their feet, and ordered them to wear shoes that were big enough for them. They hated the idea at first and thought it would ruin their chances of getting a husband. But the soldiers told them, "You can either unbind or go to prison. Please yourself, Little Sister, it is very comfortable in prison!"

In the evening the villagers would come to the inn where I stayed overnight and asked for more stories and songs.

Gradually there were ones and twos converted here and

---

there and in each village a little group gathered—the beginning of a small church. So through the next years as the gospel was preached, the practice of foot-binding ceased, opium-taking was reduced, and a witness to the saving grace of Jesus Christ was set up in many places.[142]

## PRISON RIOT

Her friendship with the mandarin is odd to consider. The respect was mutual, though they were two very different people. He was a highly learned and refined person, totally entrenched in the millennia-long tradition and civilization of China. She was a parlor maid from the streets of London with a shrill, unrefined voice who had picked up her Chinese vocabulary and speaking style from muleteers. She would come to him when she saw something that she thought needed changing. And he would tell her why it could or could not be changed. Many changes did come about through their working together.

Her relationship with the mandarin drew him to her and to her God. One day, for instance, a riot erupted in the prison. She first heard of it when the mandarin summoned her to deal with it. She was astounded. She knew nothing about prisons. But she went along to the prison and found the prison governor hovering outside the gate waiting for her. The soldiers were too afraid to deal with the criminals. It would be fair to say that Gladys was hesitant. But the prison official responded, "You preach the living God everywhere. If you preach the truth—if your God protects you from harm—then you can stop this riot."[143]

Realizing that God's reputation was at stake, she entered the prison and was stunned by what she found. Standing in the midst of dead bodies and blood, this 4-foot-10-inch woman—half the size of many of the men—grabbed an ax from the grasp of a murderer. Then she began to order hardened criminals around like a schoolmarm dealing with a bunch of naughty children. Shocked, they responded obediently. Perhaps she was the first woman they'd seen since incarceration. She was certainly the first who had spoken to them like this.

Over time, as she learned more about the situation in the prison, she was shaken by the wretched condition of the prisoners. They had

---

[142] Ibid., pp. 46-47.

[143] Alan Burgess, *The Small Woman* (Ann Arbor, Mich.: Servant Books, 1985), p. 89. This is the edition used for reference in this chapter. A newer edition is available (Cutchogue, NY: Buccaneer Books, 1993).

nothing to do and little to eat. Whether a crime was as small as forgery or as great as mass murder, all prisoners endured the same conditions. She promised them work, and eventually she got them looms and cotton and other means of occupation. Sometimes they were even allowed to come to the inn for services.

In a quiet prison after the riot was quelled, one man called to her, "Thank you, Ai-weh-deh!" She had to go home and ask someone what that meant. "The virtuous one"—that became her name.

## CITIZENSHIP

Ai-weh-deh was not just a local name she adopted to give her Chinese friends something easier on their tongues than "Gladys." It was her legal name after she became a naturalized Chinese subject. Gladys wrote, "I lived exactly like a Chinese woman. I wore Chinese clothes, ate their food, spoke their dialect, and even found myself beginning to think as they did. This was my country now; these northern Chinese were my people. I decided that I would apply to become a naturalized Chinese subject. In 1936 [four years after she arrived] my application was granted and my official name was Ai-weh-deh."[144]

This caused complications in her life as time passed. If she had retained her British citizenship, she could have been evacuated as war progressed. But as a Chinese citizen, she wasn't eligible for British assistance. This was not a complication to Gladys, though, because she didn't want to leave. China was home.

Gladys did not simply live in China. She became nearly Chinese. One young missionary couple, at least,

> were filled with admiration for this small but forceful young woman who seemed to understand everything the Chinese said, and who, sometimes to their amused alarm, did everything the Chinese did. She could spit with the best of them, and when she bit on a piece of gristle at a feast, it shot out of her mouth with utmost precision to where the dog under the table was waiting to snap it up.[145]

---

144 Aylward and Hunter, p. 48.
145 Thompson, p. 49.

Two examples nearer the end of her time in China might indicate how nearly Chinese Gladys became.

She spent her last four years in China in the city of Chengdu. Knowing that she needed a place to live, friends directed her to the China Inland Mission House. She went there, but within days, she moved into a tiny room in the courtyard of a Chinese hospital. The Christian doctor there, a Chinese man she had just met, had work she could help with. The other missionaries were astonished. "How did she get to know people in such a short time, when she arrived a perfect stranger?"[146]

Later, the Chinese pastor of a church in Chengdu appointed her as Bible Woman, a position unique to a handful of countries. "The term 'Bible women' was the common designation of Christian female nationals who were employed for a pittance by the indigenous church or by women missionaries to function as teachers, interpreters, Bible readers, and evangelists."[147] She may be the only non-Chinese who has ever worked in that capacity in China and lived the meager lifestyle that the pittance allowed. She was given a little room behind the church building and received the normal tiny allowance of a Bible woman. She became a servant of the church—a Chinese church, not a mission church. "Servant" is not a metaphor. She filled whatever roles the church and pastor required of her. One of her jobs was cleaning the church building. As she swept cobwebs and grit from every crevice, she was at the same time praying God's Spirit in and the devil out.

Although Gladys embraced life as a Chinese citizen, she once wrote, "Sometimes I longed for fellowship with someone of my own kind. I had prayed for years that someone would come out from England to share my work, but no one came, so I went on alone."[148]

## NINEPENCE AND LESS AND MORE

God never did send a Western colleague. Instead, he provided companionship in an unexpected way. One day when Gladys was on the way from the inn to the mandarin's compound, she passed a dirty, rough woman sitting beside the road. Though the woman wore silver

---

[146] Ibid., p. 109.

[147] Ruth Tucker and Walter Liefeld, *Daughters of the Church* (Grand Rapids, Mich.: Academic Books, Zondervan Publishing House, 1987), p. 340—also includes further explanation of the role and importance of Bible women.

[148] Aylward and Hunter, p. 49.

earrings and jade hairpins, the child sagging against her knee was starving, ragged, dirty, and sick. When the woman tried to sell her the child, Gladys realized this woman was one of the "devil" child sellers she had heard rumors about. Gladys turned away and continued to the mandarin's.

After performing the ritual greetings and business, she demanded to know what was being done with child-dealers. The mandarin hedged, and finally admitted that it was better to leave them alone. They were such wicked, desperate criminals that, if confronted, they would only do worse things. "About the child-dealer," he pronounced as he dismissed her, "the law says that Ai-weh-deh, the Virtuous One, is to put her head in the air and pass on the other side of the road. And you will not repeat my words to anyone!"

By protocol, he should have had the last word. But Gladys turned in the doorway. "I have to inform you, Mandarin, that I did not come to China only to observe your laws. I came for the love of Jesus Christ, and I shall act upon the principles of his teaching, no matter what you say." And she was gone. Months later the mandarin told her that was the beginning of his friendship and regard for her.[149]

Returning along the road, Gladys saw the same woman and child. "I looked at the thin, miserable, unwanted scrap of humanity and my heart ached for her sufferings. I put my hand into my pocket and found that all I possessed was five Chinese coins, about the equivalent of ninepence. I held it out."[150]

Gladys named the little girl Mei-en, Beautiful Grace, but her nickname was Ninepence. So Ninepence became her daughter and helped fill the aching void. One day Ninepence brought home a little boy who had even "less" than they did, and he became part of the family, and was called "Less." As time passed, many children were dependent on her, and she started a school for them and other children in Yangcheng. But Ninepence, Less, and just two or three others were her family for the rest of her or their lives.

## SINGLENESS

Gladys and other single women realized that a life devoted to missions probably meant life without a husband. Still, naturally, there were times

---

[149] The story of Ninepence, Less, and Bao Bao is told in Burgess, pp. 97-105.
[150] Aylward and Hunter, p. 1.

when she thought of marriage. Elisabeth Elliot recounted a conversation she had in the early 1960s with Gladys Aylward.

> She told me how she had worked happily for six or seven years in China, alone, when a missionary couple came to work nearby [a couple of days away]. She then began to ponder the privilege that was theirs, and to wonder if it might not be a lovely thing to be married. She talked to the Lord about it, asking him to call a man from England, send him straight out to China, straight to where she was, and have him propose. . . .
> "Elisabeth, I believe God answers prayer! He called him—but he never came."[151]

There was a season when things could have gone another direction. War with the Japanese brought Colonel Linnan into her life. As she and the tall, educated, handsome Chinese officer walked and talked, he revealed to her a polished facet of China she hadn't learned in the streets of rural Yangcheng. As she learned to know Linnan, she was also learning of a broader, richer side of Chinese culture. This made her realize more surely that China was indeed her own beloved country. Linnan and Gladys loved each other, and he proposed to her. She wrote her family that she planned to marry him, but she told him they must wait till the war was done. They were eventually separated by the circumstances of the war.

## WAR

Beginning in 1937 Yangcheng had heard reports of war, but it hadn't touched the remote village. Then in 1938 Yangcheng was bombed, and the Inn of the Eight Happinesses was damaged. Gladys was trapped under the rubble of one end of the inn and had to be dug out. Later she came back and found dangling on the broken wall of her room the scrap of her motto for that year, "God hath chosen the weak things—I can do all things through Christ who strengtheneth me" (1 Corinthians 1:27; Philippians 4:13).

That very hour she found God's promise true as she went out from the rubble of her inn and faced the stunned villagers. Nobody knew how to respond to such an emergency. They were in a walled town and

---

[151] Elisabeth Elliot, "Foreword," in Burgess, p. 6.

had never needed to fear attack. Yangcheng was supposed to be safe. But not when war came from the air. Gladys rallied them to remove the dead, tend the wounded, dig out the trapped. From then on Yangcheng was in a state of war.

Life as the Chinese had known it for millennia was coming to an end. After the Japanese would come the Communists and the Cultural Revolution. Of course no one could see the exact future, but the devastation of the present was clear. In the spring of 1939, the mandarin invited Gladys to a feast, saying, "It will probably be the last ever held in the town of Yangcheng, as we are leaving little that is useful. I have something to say I wish you to hear."

Gladys was surprised to find herself seated in the place of honor at the mandarin's right hand. She had been to many feasts during her seven years in Yangcheng and was used to being the only woman, but she had never been given the seat of honor. Around her were all the most important people of the town. As the climax of the evening, the mandarin spoke of Ai-weh-deh's work among them, of her care for the sick and the prisoners, of her Christian faith that they had so often talked about. After several minutes of praise for Gladys, he turned to her and announced that he wanted to embrace her faith and become a Christian.

From the mandarin down, all levels of society in the area had been touched by the God of Gladys Aylward. One mule driver was ordered by Japanese soldiers to carry their ammunition. He refused because as a Christian and pacifist, he couldn't assist their fighting. Because of his Christian stand, they tied him to a post within sight and sound of his home, blocked the doors of the house, and burned it to the ground with his wife and children inside.

Gladys's story for the next couple of years of war is a cycle of fleeing war and returning—fleeing to cave villages in the mountains, returning home, moving to a mission station in Tsechow or elsewhere, then coming back to Yangcheng.

In spite of the continuing and unpredictable danger, Gladys did not want to leave China. During the darkest months of the war, her mother received a letter that spoke from the true heart of Gladys Aylward:

> Life is pitiful, death so familiar, suffering and pain so common,
> yet I would not be anywhere else. Do not wish me out of this

or in any way seek to get me out, for I will not be got out while this trial is on. These are my people, God has given them to me, and I will live or die with them for him and his glory.[152]

Her life was so far removed from England that she did not know until 1941 that Europe had been at war since 1939. It was during this time more than any other that she sensed special direction and protection from God.

## PROTECTION

Once, for example, while walking alone along the track between Yangcheng and the mountain cave hideaways, she sensed danger, but didn't know what to do. She prayed, "Oh, Lord, please decide for me; please make me choose the right way." She shut her eyes and spun around, opened her eyes and started in the direction she was pointing, straight up the steep, stony mountainside. Within a few moments she heard Japanese troops coming along the very path where she would have been trapped.

Sometimes God warned her through other people. She was with other missionaries when they heard of the Japanese taking a city nearby. She and others were ready to pack and run. Annie Skau was a young Norwegian missionary who ordinarily took directions and was not a pushy person. But this time she was firm. "I do not think the Lord wants us to go. He has spoken to me. He has given me his word. I was not looking for it—it was in the place where I was reading this morning. 'Behold, I will send a blast upon him, and he shall hear a rumour and return to his own land.' . . . I do not think we should run." The missionaries prayed and decided to stay, and the Japanese began to retreat because of the reports of military actions elsewhere.

Sometimes God guided her directly through Scripture. She learned the Japanese were offering a hundred dollars for her capture. It was her love of China that had opened her to Japanese accusations of spying, because as she trekked from village to village and detected Japanese activity, she felt justified in passing the information to the Chinese Nationalist forces. Now with a price on her head, some friends urged her to flee, while others begged her not to leave them. She had no idea

---

[152] Burgess, p. 149.

what to do. Then she read in her Bible, "Flee ye; flee ye into the mountains; dwell deeply in hidden places, because the king of Babylon has conceived a purpose against you."[153] She ran through gunfire to safety. She was away from home at the time, and so she returned to Yangcheng.

## FLIGHT WITH 100 CHILDREN

In Yangcheng, in the crumbling Inn of Eight Happinesses, she was greeted by about 100 children who had been led to refuge in Yangcheng from a mission orphanage in another town. Gladys knew it wouldn't be long before the Japanese would look for her there, so she could not stay. Because of war, it was harder and harder to provide for children, but in order to protect them, she knew she couldn't leave them behind.

She had received word that an orphanage in Xian would care for them—if she could get them there. By early 1940, one group of 100 had already gone with a co-worker. But the roads had still been open then. Now, when Gladys needed to go, the roads were not safe because of troop movements.

The next morning she said farewell forever to the Inn of the Eight Happinesses and to Yangcheng, which had been her home for eight years. In later years, when asked where she was from, she answered, "Yangcheng," so unquestionably had that become home.

She led a line of children away from the town, each carrying his or her own blanket and bowl and chopsticks. The mandarin, as his last good-bye to Gladys, gave them what he could—enough food for two days. And just as God provided through the mandarin, he continued to give them what they needed each day—food some days, hunger some. Over mountains and rough, narrow paths they trekked, avoiding all roads, because of the soldiers there.

A Buddhist priest invited them to sleep one night in an almost-deserted temple. A man they met in the mountains asked them into his courtyard to sleep. Other nights they slept in the open. For the first few days it was like an adventure, an extended picnic. Then their cloth shoes began to wear through, and their feet became sore and bloody. They were filthy and had run out of food. Suddenly, seven nights out,

---

[153] This is the way she remembered Jeremiah 49:30 as she looked back to that event. Another reason for the difference in the quote is that she was reading from a Chinese Bible, which she continued to do even when she returned to Britain. When she read to an audience, she would do an instant mental translation from Chinese to English.

soldiers came upon them. Panic gave way to relief when they recognized Chinese Nationalist forces. About fifty soldiers camped with them and shared the food from their knapsacks. Everyone slept better that night. Perhaps it was a slight respite before the rigors to come. Sometimes the rock faces were so steep they had to hand the youngest ones down one by one. The sun beat down on them, and they needed to rest every few hundred yards. By now Gladys and the older children were carrying the blankets of the little ones, and there were piggyback rides as long as the older children could bear the weight. Gladys held before them the hope of reaching the village of Yuan Chu, near the Yellow River. "We'll have food there!"

## BUT GOD IS GOD

After twelve long days, they staggered into Yuan Chu and found it deserted. Everyone had fled for fear of the Japanese. And there were no boats to take them across the massive Yellow River, because that's how the villagers had escaped to the other side.

Gladys and the exhausted children sat beside the river for four days, getting hungrier and hungrier. Gladys was beginning to feel ill and could see no hope. This seemed the end of the road. The enemy would hem them in here and capture them, or worse.

Thirteen-year-old Sualan interrupted Gladys's nightmare daydreams: "Ai-weh-deh, do you remember telling us how Moses took the children of Israel to the waters of the Red Sea? And how God commanded the water to open and the Israelites crossed in safety?"

"Yes, I remember," Gladys replied.

"Then why doesn't God open the waters of the Yellow River for us to cross?"

In Gladys's answer, we hear the answer any weary mother might have given. "I am not Moses, Sualan."

"But God is always God, Ai-weh-deh. You have told us so a hundred times. If he is God He can open the river for us."[154]

Shamed, Gladys prayed with the children, still seeing no way that God could help them here.

A Chinese officer, patrolling the banks, heard singing and was perplexed, because he thought no one was left on this side of the river. He

---

[154] Burgess, pp. 224-225.

was astounded to discover a small foreign woman, looking ill, sitting in the midst of 100 Chinese children. They would die if they stayed, because this would soon be a battlefield. But he had the authority to commandeer a boat from the other side to take them over. He whistled a shrill, peculiar signal. And two men on the other side began to row toward them. After three trips across, all the children were on the other side.

At the village on the other side, Gladys was arrested because she had crossed the Yellow River. It was impossible and illegal to cross the Yellow River now; so since she crossed it, the authorities assumed she must be a spy. In her weary state, Gladys must have felt like she was delirious. She was in this village because she was fleeing the Japanese who wanted her because she was a spy for the Chinese, and now the Chinese were accusing her of spying for Japan. As she was being examined, the children stood outside chanting, "Let her out! Let her out!" When the magistrate realized that arresting Gladys meant taking over the care of 100 children, he found his way clear to let her go.

From there Gladys and the children traveled four days by a refugee train. When it seemed impossible to make it over an imposing mountain pass, God provided a train where there was supposed to be none. The children, who had no idea what a train was, were at first terrified by the giant hissing, roaring, whistling monster. It was a coal train, and the children slept on it through the night, riding on top of the piles of coal.

By now, all was a blur to Gladys. Even when she woke somewhat refreshed from a night's sleep, she was weaker. She couldn't remember how much time they had spent in the village at the end of the coal train's route. She couldn't remember how many days the ride was to Xian.

When fever had almost captured her, then came the last, greatest blow. The gates of Xian were closed to refugees. There was no more room. She leaned her hot, heavy head against the wall, despairing. All this way they had come! What would become of her children? She hardly had strength to rejoice when she discovered there was a place at Fufeng, a nearby village. In a daze, she and the children traveled there by yet another train.

Almost as soon as she delivered her children safely into the hands of other caregivers at Fufeng, she collapsed with typhus and relapsing fever. For more than two weeks, she slipped between delirium and unconsciousness. No one knew who this small woman was, raving wildly in fluent, street Chinese.

## GOOD-BYE

While she was recuperating, Colonel Linnan found her after months of searching and wondering where she was. They were together again, and the war was over. She had been so sure back in Shanxi that with the end of the war they could marry. He begged her to marry him, but things looked different now to Gladys. Alan Burgess explains it by saying:

> Now, instead of that inner exultation, the rounded delight of knowing that she loved and was loved in return, here was this nagging anxiety to do the right thing by her God, her children, and the man she loved.
>
> Somewhere in the mountains between Yancheng and the Yellow River, somewhere on the plains between the Yellow River and the old capital of Sian, somewhere in the unreal world of delirium and the fevers of her illness, certitude had been replaced by anxiety.[155]

They said good-bye and never saw each other again.

The uncertainty and anxiety she felt with Linnan seemed to be a new ingredient in Gladys Aylward after that. Some strength or stability seemed to have been burned away by the fever and war and the destruction all around her in her beloved China. Perhaps her sense of rootlessness was due to losing her home in Yangcheng. She never again seemed to belong anywhere in the same way she had belonged there. She never lost her roots in God and in her Savior Jesus, but she became transient in almost every other way.

## TRANSIENT

One of her biographers said that when people said, "Come any time—just let us know how we can help," she took them at their word. She'd turn up unannounced: "It's me." "Rather like a child sure of a welcome,

---

[155] Ibid., pp. 251-252.

staying for a while, then disappearing again, back among the Chinese."[156]

Until the end, her friends could detect the flavor of loneliness in Gladys, the independent woman.

> Perhaps it was having someone to talk to in her own tongue that meant more to [Gladys] than anything. "When Mrs. Jeffery knows Gladys Aylward's coming she just puts everything aside and gets out her knitting!" chuckled the young missionaries who were living there while they did their language study. "Mrs. Jeffery knits and smiles, and Gladys talks and talks! It's a life-saver for her."
>
> One day she went along with a large birthday card. "I want you all to sign it," [Gladys] said, "My mum thinks I'm here all alone, without any friends, and this will cheer her up no end." But after a few hours she disappeared again, back among the Chinese, back to the tiny room with a bed and a table and a chest of drawers and a chair or two—and that huge thermos flask in which to keep hot water to provide her and her guests with drinks for the day.[157]

When Gladys regained some of her health, she moved to a remote mountain village near Lanchow, the city mentioned in the magazine story that first drew her heart to China. She lived there a year, teaching new Christians. Then she felt God calling her to Chengdu in Szechuan Province. This is where she was appointed to be a humble Bible Woman, performing the duties of a servant for her Chinese church there. She stayed four years in Chengdu.

## HOME

In 1949 Gladys returned to England with the financial help of friends. She had always thought she'd live in China till she died. For one thing, she had no money to travel. Her parents didn't recognize her when she stepped off the train. Someone had to point them toward her—the small Chinese woman standing bewildered beside her bags.

She remained in Britain for several years, but she yearned for

---

156 Thompson, p. 94.
157 Ibid., p. 110.

China. Since the Communists were now in control, she couldn't return to the mainland. So she moved to Formosa (Taiwan), the only Chinese place open to her, where God led her into a ministry with orphans.

The parlor maid Gladys Aylward had not felt at home in England. In Yangcheng, she settled down and had a home, but it was not a permanent one, and eventually it was taken from her. Nowhere felt like home after that. But her true, eternal home was waiting. On New Year's Day, 1970, Gladys Aylward moved from Taipei to the place that her Jesus had been preparing for her. Her body was buried in Taipei, but she lives now in the home that she will never have to leave.

Gladys Aylward was only four feet, ten inches. She was a poor student and quit school at fourteen. She had a shrill, immature voice, no money, and no backing from a mission board. She was truly a weak thing—about the least thing we can think of—to go to China. But she found God to be strong and faithful to his word. "God chose what is weak—I can do all things through him who strengthens me."

Did the mission board make a mistake when they rejected her application? We can't really know the answer to that question. But it seems unlikely to me that she would have been successful working within the bounds of a conventional mission agency. We do know that God had plans to send her to China, and he used an unconventional way, a way that fit her and prepared her.

For instance, who would ever have imagined that a parlor maid could have enough money for train fare to China? Nowadays, most missionary candidates receive advice from their mission boards about how to find people who will be interested in their ministries and who, therefore, will pray and perhaps make financial donations. Gladys, on the contrary, was cast onto her own devices—working at her job and at extra jobs to earn and save. But no! She wasn't on her own; she cast herself onto God and learned his provision.

For a missionary candidate now, in the whirlwind of letters, visits, biblical teaching, and presentations about future ministry—the activities that will raise interest and money—sometimes it might be easy to lose clear sight of the true source of the support. And missionaries aren't the only ones who may lean too heavily on their own skill, persistence, and charisma. Any of us might depend so much on our skills, diligence, and seniority that we forget Jesus' words in Matthew 6:31-33:

> *Therefore do not be anxious, saying, "What shall we eat?" or "What shall we drink?" or "What shall we wear?" For the Gentiles seek after all these things, and your heavenly Father knows that you need them all. But seek first the kingdom of God and his righteousness, and all these things will be added to you.*

Whether he provides for us through our hard work or through the gifts of missions supporters, we have nothing without him.

God is the one who gives every one of us life and breath and everything (Acts 17:25). Not just money and food. *Everything!* I ask myself and you: What is it that keeps us from venturing into something that God has been putting in front of us? What is it that causes us to say, "I can't possibly do that." What am I afraid of? What do I lack? What are my weaknesses?

Gladys Aylward had every reason to say she couldn't go to China. She could not have afforded it. She could not have survived the trip through Russia. She could not have led 100 children safely across the mountains and the Yellow River. No, *she* couldn't. But God could.

If we think we can't do what God is asking us to do, we're right. But God *can*.

In spite of the inauspicious beginnings of the life of Gladys Aylward and the inauspicious person she seemed to be, she could look back at the end of her life to see how God had worked through her. There was her own small family of adopted children, and in southern Shanxi Province there were hundreds of orphans whose lives had been saved and who had received some formal education. Many of them had also been saved spiritually. She could foresee the end of foot-binding. Productive changes had been made for prisoners. She could remember sick people who had been healed and babies she had helped to birth. A traditional mandarin was now her brother, and believers and churches were scattered in villages throughout the most remote mountains.

*With my map of China before me, I follow the route of Gladys's life. Her home, Yangcheng, is in Shanxi (Shansi), the province where I visited friends a few years ago. They took me to an orphanage whose 100 children still await their deliverer. Other friends are scattered around the country, all having followed God's call there, as Gladys did. And so this story of Gladys Aylward is dedicated to my friends who are (or have been) in China for the sake of the gospel. As they would wish, I won't name them. But God knows who they are.*

*N*ebuchadnezzar answered and said to them, "Is it true,
O Shadrach, Meshach, and Abednego, that you do not
serve my gods or worship the golden image that I have set up?
Now if you are ready when you hear the sound of the horn,
pipe, lyre, trigon, harp, bagpipe, and every kind of music,
to fall down and worship the image that I have made,
well and good. But if you do not worship,
you shall immediately be cast into a burning fiery furnace.
And who is the god who will deliver you out of my hands?"

*S*hadrach, Meshach, and Abednego answered and said to the king,
"O Nebuchadnezzar, we have no need to answer you in this matter.
If this be so, our God whom we serve is able to deliver us from
    the burning fiery furnace,
and he will deliver us out of your hand, O king.
But if not, be it known to you, O king,
that we will not serve your gods
or worship the golden image that you have set up."

DANIEL 3:14-18

# ESTHER AHN KIM

## (AHN EI SOOK OR AHN I SOOK)

*Faithful in Suffering*

⟨∞⟩

In the early 1900s, American Indian children in many parts of the United States were taken from their homes and sent to boarding schools, sometimes hundreds of miles away. Their long hair was cut. Their traditional clothes were taken away and replaced with standardized "modern" clothes. They were given European-American names. They were required to use only English and punished for speaking Ojibwe, Navajo, or Cherokee. In the decades before this, the parents and grandparents of these children had been relocated to reservations, their homes and lands confiscated.

There were white Americans who did not agree with these Americanization efforts. But for too many years, the American government's policies prevailed.

In the early 1900s, on the other side of the globe, Japan went to war against Russia to liberate Korea from the occupying Russian troops. In those days, there was one Korean nation—not North Korea and South Korea, as there are now. At first, Koreans welcomed the Japanese because they seemed kinder than the Russians. But the welcome didn't last because the mirage of brotherhood didn't last.

Then in the 1930s, when Japan occupied Manchuria and began all-out war with China, Korea became a strategic geographical link. Through Korea, Japan had an overland route into Manchuria and China. And so they intensified their grasp on Korea by carrying out a major Japanization campaign. This is why many Koreans refer to 1937-1945 as the Dark Age.

Japanese authorities confiscated whatever they wanted, from food to facilities. Nearly all young Korean men and women were conscripted to work in war camps. Everyone was required to speak Japanese. Speaking Korean was a punishable offense. Koreans were ordered to drop their family names and take Japanese names. Compliance was high, because noncompliance meant no job for adults and no school for children.

There were Japanese Christians and others who did not agree with the Japanese government's actions. But for too many years, the Japanese government's policies prevailed.

## BE A GREAT PERSON

Early in the occupation, in the town of Bhak Chon, a child was born. This was not the child a traditional Korean father would have longed for. First of all, she was a girl. And besides, she was so small and thin that the relatives ridiculed her. Her father, though, looked down at his frail firstborn and murmured, "Poor baby. Don't die, but be a great person."[158] The family's name was Ahn, and the child was named Ei Sook.[159]

Ei Sook's father was the firstborn of his parents. So when his wife bore him only daughters, there was stress amongst the family: He *needed* an heir. So he gave in to the pressure for sons and took many concubines.

Ei Sook's mother was the daughter of a high government official in Seoul. She had accepted Christ when she was eight. Because she had neither church nor Bible, she remembered and lived by the four principles the missionary had taught her:

1. Jesus is the only Son of God and is the only Savior.

2. Jesus will never forsake his believers.

3. Jesus is able to take all the misfortunes of believers and turn them into good.

4. Jesus hears the prayers of his children.

From the beginning of Ei Sook's life, her mother was her strong support. Her words seemed to be like God's voice, sometimes gentle and comforting, often firm and spine-stiffening, always what Ei Sook needed at the moment.

In contrast, the matriarch of the household, Ei Sook's paternal grandmother, was always discontented and complaining. The child could see that her grandmother's idols—her gods—brought her no

---

[158] Esther Ahn Kim, *If I Perish* (Chicago: Moody Press, 1977), p. 228. I have told only a fraction of Ahn Ei Sook's story. I encourage people to read this book for a fuller account.

[159] Esther Ahn Kim was her American married name.

happiness. In fact, they seemed to be at the root of the misery. Once Ei Sook sneaked into the storage room where dishes of food were waiting to be offered to the gods at a coming festival. She cried out to the idols, "You devils! Why do you eat the best foods and then make my grandmother unhappy? Die eating the food mixed with my spittle!" Then she spat on her finger and rubbed each of the foods with it.[160]

Her mother and sister and other Christians began to watch to see what would become of this headstrong little girl. Already Ei Sook's mother was pointing her to the true God: "As you can see, idols have no power at all. The Lord Jesus is the only One who can give us true power and happiness and peace."[161]

As an adult, Ei Sook remembered the difference between her mother and her grandmother:

> [My mother] was one of those persons who always lived for others. Once a week she filled a sack with aspirin, salve, candy, and tissue paper and visited the poor. I had never seen her eat warm rice. She would always cook a large amount of rice at one time.
>
> "If I have plenty of cooked rice," she told me when I asked her about it, "I can give some to a beggar when he comes. In order to follow Jesus, I think we should always be prepared to give to others."
>
> Mother was so different from the other members of my father's household. They only gave away that which they did not want to keep for themselves. They seemed to hate each other and only lived from day to day. They had no God, no holy day, no true joy or confidence. Wherever Mother was, it was like a chapel of heaven around her.[162]

## ONE PERSON WITH TRUE FAITH

When Ei Sook was young, her mother left her father and his concubines and his family and moved to Pyongyang. Ei Sook's father still oversaw her education and required her to attend exclusive Japanese-speaking schools. Afterward her mother wanted to send her to America

---

[160] Kim, p. 95.
[161] Ibid., p. 96.
[162] Ibid., p. 144.

to a Christian college, but her father insisted that she go to university in Japan.

But over all, her mother's daily godly influence far surpassed her father's impact on her life.

> We used to get up at four in the morning and go to church together to pray. . . . We walked in silence until we came to a Japanese shrine along the road. My mother stopped suddenly and looked toward heaven. Then she stomped the ground and said, "Perish and disappear! In the name of Jesus Christ who has risen from the dead to live forever." She repeated those words three times. On the way from church, she would do the same thing.
>
> "Mother," I said to her, "the Japanese now have all of Korea within their shrine, and their nation is among the strongest in all the world. What do you think just one person can do?"
>
> "In God's sight," she said quietly, "one person with true faith in Him is far more important than a thousand without faith. Abraham and Moses and David all stood alone. They were called and served God as individuals. I believe God is the same today."
>
> The words of 2 Chronicles [16:9] were surely true, I thought. "For the eyes of Jehovah run to and fro throughout the whole earth, to show himself strong in the behalf of them whose heart is perfect toward him."[163]

## THE DILEMMA

For Ei Sook's family, as for all Koreans, the Japanese occupation brought financial hardship, grief, and cultural confusion. But the great *moral* dilemma was caused by one regulation in particular—the requirement that everyone participate in ceremonies at Shinto shrines.

Here was the dilemma for Christians. If a person bowed before a shrine, was that a religious observation or was it simply political expedience? Within each shrine stood an image of the Japanese sun goddess and a picture of the emperor of Japan. Bowing is a traditional Eastern sign of respect. So bowing before the emperor's picture might

---

[163] Ibid., pp. 146-147.

be simply a sign of respect and patriotism—not willingly granted by an oppressed Korean, of course—but still, he'd just be going through political motions. In order to justify this as only a political act, the Korean would have to ignore the goddess image or relegate it to the status of a mere cultural figure.

On the other hand, if bowing includes the sun goddess within its circle of reverence, the event becomes a spiritual, religious occasion. What raised the stakes even higher was the historic reality that, until the end of World War II, the emperor was considered by most Japanese to be a divine being—a god.

By 1940, most foreign missionaries had left Korea, partly because Koreans had been forbidden to have contact with foreigners. So the missionaries' local friends would be endangered by any interaction with them. But the Shinto shrine issue was the main reason they left. Japan was putting pressure on all church leaders, including missionaries, to lead their people to the shrines.

Shrines had been built in every city and village. Miniatures had been placed in every government office and school. Schoolchildren were given tiny shrines to take home and told to worship daily. There was no escaping the demand of the shrine. Finally, they were even put in Christian churches. Police were on hand at every gathering to make sure everyone bowed at the shrine before Christian services began. Anyone who refused was arrested. Pastors were watched especially closely because of the influence they would have on their congregation. Insubordinate pastors or those deemed to have a bad attitude were arrested and tortured, and their family's food ration was cut off.

Some denominational groups agreed quickly to comply with shrine attendance, explaining to their people that this was simply patriotic. Other denominations held out longer, but finally couldn't bear the pressure. Some hoped that God would overlook their shrine attendance since they were forced to it by the Japanese. But in spite of leadership capitulation, a large number of people within the churches would not bow. Those who were in public and leadership positions bore the brunt of the government's retribution.

## BUT IF NOT . . .

In 1939, when the issue had come to a head, Ahn Ei Sook was the music teacher in a Christian school for girls in the city of Pyongyang.

The day had come when every student and every teacher was required to attend the rally of schools at the shrine at Namsan Mountain in the center of the city of Seoul.

Her principal would suffer unless everyone in the school complied. But Ei Sook remembered the words of Jesus: "*I am the way, and the truth, and the life*" (John 14:6). How could she bow before an idol?

When pressed by the principal, she unwillingly agreed to go to the mountain. But she could not promise to bow once she was there. As the principal continued her persuasion, Ei Sook was very aware that her students were listening and watching. They knew that her conscience was against bowing. Now they would see if her actions corresponded to her words. She thought of the defiant, confident words of Shadrach, Meshach, and Abednego.

*Our God whom we serve is able to deliver us from the burning fiery furnace, and he will deliver us out of your hand, O king. But if not, be it known to you, O King, that we will not serve your gods or worship the golden image that you have set up.*

DANIEL 3:17-18

Ei Sook knew that even if one does what is right, there is no guarantee that God will respond with immediate safety.

"But if not." Even if God didn't save them from the burning fire, they would die honoring him. I was going to make the same decision. With God's help, I would never bow before the Japanese idol, even if He did not save me from the hands of the Japanese. I was saved by Jesus. I could bow only before God, the Father of my Savior. I felt as though I could already see the burning furnace yawning for me.

While we walked I was praying. I knew what I was going to do. "Today on the mountain, before the large crowd," I told myself, "I will proclaim that there is no other God beside you. This is what I will do for Your holy name."[164]

For a few moments she was filled with peace. Then, alternating

---

[164] Ibid., p. 14.

between that peace and a great sense of weakness and fear, she arrived with her students at the mountain.

> I was like a child at the shrine, afraid even to make a noise because of the police officers. As a sense of uneasiness swept over me, I tried to pray, but my prayers were too weak. . . . I stammered out my own lack of courage and strength. "O Lord," I prayed, "I am so weak! But I am your sheep so I must obey and follow You. Lord, watch over me."[165]

In answer, God brought to her mind words that were stored in her heart and memory: "My sheep hear my voice, and I know them, and they follow me" (John 10:27).

## PROFOUNDEST BOW TO . . .

The scene was reminiscent of ancient Babylon, when the multitude, including all the foreign captives, were gathered and waiting for the musical signal to bow before King Nebuchadnezzar's monstrous golden image.[166]

> "Attention!" A strident order shrilled above the murmuring of the crowd. The people straightened, line by line. We were accustomed to being subservient, for we had been the captives of the Japanese for more than thirty-seven years. "Our profoundest bow to Amaterasu Omikami [the sun goddess]!"
> As one person, that enormous crowd followed the shouted order by bending the upper half of their bodies solemnly and deeply. Of all the people at the shrine, I was the only one who remained erect, looking straight at the sky. [167]

Ei Sook was not naïve. Being a teacher meant she was a leader, and leaders were watched by the officials. Now, in her obedience to God, she had singled herself out as disobedient to the occupying authorities. The weak, thin baby had grown into a fragile, sickly woman—not a likely candidate to withstand the suffering and torturing that she knew

---

[165] Ibid., p. 15.
[166] Daniel 3.
[167] Kim, pp. 15-16.

would lie ahead. Walking away from the shrine, she thought, *I am dead. Ahn Ei Sook died today at mountain Namsan.*[168]

> I could honestly say I was not afraid of dying, but I feared being tortured without dying. How long could this body endure? What if I gave up my faith under the relentless torture? Just thinking of it made me so faint I could hardly see where I was walking. . . .
>
> "Let not your heart be troubled," Jesus was saying to me. "Believe in God, believe also in me. . . . I will not leave you desolate. . . . Peace I leave with you; my peace I give to you. . . . Let not your heart be troubled, neither let it be fearful" (John 14:1, 18, 27).
>
> A light was turned on in the darkness of my heart. . . . And a song came to mind.
>
> > *Did we in our own strength confide,*
> > *Our striving would be losing;*
> > *Were not the right Man on our side,*
> > *The Man of God's own choosing:*
> > *Dost ask who that may be?*
> > *Christ Jesus it is He; Lord Sabaoth his Name,*
> > *From age to age the same,*
> > *And He must win the battle.*
> > —MARTIN LUTHER[169]

Four detectives were waiting in her classroom. Her students watched as the men took her away. She writes, "My fear of suffering was transformed into the thrill of starting some splendid adventure. My mind was calm."[170]

She was taken to the office of the chief of the district. Before he could deal with her, he received a phone call and hurried away. When he stepped away, Ei Sook walked out of his office and ran home. Christians had already gathered to pray for her. Her mother helped her disguise herself with dirt and old clothes. She grabbed a seat in the first train leaving the station and ended up in Shin Ei Joo, in the far north, near the Manchurian border.

---

[168] Ibid., p. 18.
[169] Ibid., pp. 16-17.
[170] Ibid., p. 19.

She wept and prayed in the cold, despairing at the prospect of enduring the frigidity of a prison cell someday. In fear and loneliness she called to God for help. At that very moment she remembered that a former student lived in this town. She stayed with the student for a short time and then traveled on to her sister's home in Jung Loo.

## PREPARING TO SUFFER

Ei Sook was thrilled to see that their mother had come from Pyongyang and was waiting for her. Her mother knew Ei Sook's weakness. But she also knew the strength of God, and so she did not try to shield Ei Sook from suffering. Rather, she helped her prepare for it.

> I always felt strengthened when I talked with Mother about God and His love. I began to think that life might be worth living in this time of persecution. It might even be a truer picture of the believer to agonize, to suffer, to be hated, and tortured, and even to be killed in obeying God's words rather than to live an ordinary, uneventful life.[171]

The two of them found a deserted, isolated small house. Ei Sook's sister was afraid for them to move there because someone in that house had died of tuberculosis. Ei Sook responded, "One day I will become a prisoner and will die in a cell somewhere. Do you think it is only two or three who have died from tuberculosis in jail? In this house I will prepare myself to go to that merciless jail."[172]

Her mother was exactly the companion she needed as she hid away. In this place God would provide a retreat where Ei Sook could be refreshed and strengthened, and together they could prepare for what lay ahead.

Living in that house, she soaked up the serenity and strength of the brook and field and woods and sky around her. Rainstorms and powerful weather seemed to energize her. Because they were isolated, she could sing hymns loudly. During the weeks they were there, she memorized many hymns and more than 100 chapters of the Bible. For years to come, this would be the last feast of open spaces, nature, and sweet isolation.

---

[171] Ibid., pp. 27-28.
[172] Ibid., p. 28.

But alongside the strengthening sweetness, her preparation was for hard things. She slept without a quilt. She had midnight visits from persecuted Christians who were hiding out in the mountains, and she heard their nerve-wracking stories.

> I knew it would be impossible for me to keep my faith in my own power. God would have to work through me if I was to stand firm. I decided to fast.[173]

She fasted for longer and longer periods. After a week-long fast with no food *or drink*, she says,

> Although I had not expected it, after the fast I was able to understand the Scriptures better and I felt a new power in my prayer. Now I felt that I could leave the fear of torture in the Lord's hands.[174]

But fear could not be exterminated once and for all. When she fell into anxiety again, she decided to fast for ten days.

> Those ten days were ten months to me. The color of my eyes changed, and my breath became so offensive that nobody would come near me. My blood circulation was so low and weak that I was sure that, this time, I would die. I am quite sure that I was very close to death.
>     "O Lord," I kept telling Him, "this is so much better than torture."[175]

## FLIGHT

When her sister ran to them with the news that the Japanese knew where she was, she had to flee again, staying one place and another. As Ei Sook left her mother, she realized that it is not only the persecuted ones who lean on God for strength.

---

[173] Ibid., p. 34.
[174] Ibid.
[175] Ibid., p. 35.

It was hard for Mother to see me leave. . . . The tears flowed as I thought of Mother, who was left alone now with her aching heart. She would be even more dependent upon the Lord than before.[176]

Wherever Ei Sook was during these days of hiding, she saw and heard everything in the light of the torture she expected in the future. When she had an uncharacteristic and excruciating headache for days, she thought that the pain of torture might be like that. When she was staying next door to a hospital for a few days, the moans of the suffering soaked into her, and she felt like she was in hell—or prison. When a room she slept in was filthy and putrid, she compared it to what she could expect in a jail cell.

Then one night, alone and far away from home, she was awakened as if someone had spoken: "Go to Pyongyang." But no one else was to be seen. She had been wandering, wondering what was next. This was God's *first pointer* toward the specific path that was waiting for her. She followed his voice and headed back to Pyongyang.

She experienced the *second pointer* toward God's path when she got off the train in Pyongyang. A train full of Japanese soldiers had just arrived. Her eye was caught by their solemn, blank faces.

The soldiers all had that strange look of death, as though they were being sent to hell for the sake of the state. . . . Someone must save these tens of thousands of fine young men from the road to hell.

I stomped the ground and cried in my frustration and anger. If only someone in a high position would stand up to the Japanese leaders and make them see that the youth from all over the country were turning into fiends in hell, day after day. . . . That burden tormented me like a fire that would not be quenched. Then suddenly I heard a voice speaking to my heart, "You are the one! You must do it!"[177]

## PREPARING TO DIE

She discovered that her mother was in Pyongyang waiting for her. She told her mother about the experience at the train station.

---

[176] Ibid., p. 38.
[177] Ibid., pp. 47-48.

Her reaction was startling to me. "The time has come for you to prepare yourself to die," she said.

Death was coming for me! . . . I had to prepare myself for imprisonment; I had to practice to die.[178]

The first step was to learn to live in deep poverty. She and her mother moved into a house near the open market. It was not considered proper for ladies of their class and education even to visit the market. But each day they were there, handing out tracts and trying to tell people about Jesus. And each day in their house they continued the disciplines they had begun in the country: prayer, hymns—quietly now—worshiping, and memorizing Scripture.

She made a habit of buying complete lots of poor produce from the poorest venders—at full price. Then she culled through and gave what was edible to her mother and sister. She ate what was left. She was preparing for the rotten beans and millet she expected in prison.

Another sort of prison preparation was added as they discovered and were discovered by "wanted criminals"—Christians who were hiding around the city. They met secretly at night in a remote house.

We fasted as a group and made it a habit to eat as plainly as possible and to sleep without using quilts. Although we were all poor, we were never in want, and our houses and clothes were clean. We were all filled with the Holy Spirit and were convinced it was more than an honor to die for the Lord. We constantly lived in fear of the police, but we were happy and satisfied, envying no one. Having prayed all night, Pastor Power Chae would often stand up in joy, dancing and singing, while tears ran down his cheeks.

For us it was a joyous blessing to have been born in such a place and for such a time. I realized that it was because of this persecution that I was able to truly experience God's presence and trust His promises.[179]

She and others visited with pastors who had recently been released from prison. They hoped to know more about what to expect and to

---

178 Ibid., p. 50.
179 Ibid., p. 53.

gain strength for what lay ahead. They longed to hear that God would intervene with a miracle when torture escalated beyond bearing. But the answer itself was almost torture.

> "The cruel whip tears the flesh," [Pastor Joo] said as casually as though he were describing a walk in the park. "My nerves felt as though they were being burned by fire. The only way of escaping was to faint. I have no idea how much torture is awaiting us, but do not expect a miracle to spare you. Men killed Christ on the cross in the same way."
>
> [Ei Sook continues.] I was struck dumb, as though I had been clubbed. I cried until I thought I could cry no more.[180]

## THE PATH GOD HAS POINTED TOWARD

Then came the *third pointer* toward the particular pathway to which God was sending her. An old man arrived at their house one morning. He was Elder Park. Like Ei Sook, he had heard God. His directions were even more specific—"The time has come to choose selected soldiers of Christ. Go to Pyongyang and find Miss Ahn."[181]

Remembering the blank-faced soldiers at the train station, she asked Elder Park what God wanted him to do.

Elder Park said, "God wants to warn the Japanese. You are an excellent speaker in their language, but when I first saw you I knew that you are weak in your faith."[182]

And she was. She knew that Elder Park was right: God had called her to go to Japan with his message, but she confessed that she was very afraid.

"You need not be. God will surely hide us and blind their eyes. The Bible is the promise of power of the living God. What does it say? God is my refuge. God will hide us from enemies."[183] She said later,

> This old man brought a quiet change in me. I had been trying like a fanatic to obtain a solution simply by fasting for the persecution which I knew was coming to me. What an honorable

---

[180] Ibid., p. 54.
[181] Ibid., p. 57.
[182] Ibid., p. 58.
[183] Ibid.

privilege it would be if such a worthless one as I would be able to die for the Lord! Now I felt the time had come. . . . The difference between this old man and the other believers I knew was that he was dashing toward death while we were waiting for it.[184]

No one looking at her life would have agreed that she was just *waiting* for death. They would have seen how much preparation she was making for imprisonment and death. But maybe that's what she meant. Elder Park wasn't *preparing* for death, he was diving right into it.

Battling fiercely inside, she got up out of a pneumonia sickbed and put on her best clothes and went downtown to look for a sign. She stood in an obvious place and bowed her head. She told the Lord, "If the people suddenly stop and look at me in surprise, I will believe that you have given my face a special glow. *Then* I will follow your voice unto death and go to Japan."[185] She opened her eyes and saw that nobody was paying her the slightest attention. So perhaps this was God's sign that she should not go to Japan.

At home, her mother was understanding, but firm. "You want to do what the Bible does not say. Jonah did not pray for a sign before he went to Nineveh. Esther did not ask for a sign before she approached the king. It is wrong and dangerous to ask God for what the Bible does not say. The Bible is our guide."[186]

## IF I PERISH, I PERISH

After a three-day fast, from her Bible one passage glowed brightly— again God was giving her his own word as her guide.

Son of man, stand on your feet . . . . I am sending you to . . . a rebellious people who have rebelled against me; they . . . are stubborn and obstinate children; and you shall say to them, "Thus says the Lord God." Ezekiel 2:1ff.[187]

She would go, and she was sure that she would die at the hands of the Japanese.

---

[184] Ibid., p. 59.
[185] Ibid., pp. 60-61.
[186] Ibid., p. 61.
[187] Ibid.

Now seeing her determination to follow God's leading, her mother said, "Concerning your going to warn the Japanese authorities, I can think of many things that make me feel that God has planned this for you since you were a child."[188]

Because of her education in Japan, she was fluent in Japanese. She had made friends in Japan and felt at home there. In earlier days, she had gone back to visit as often as she could. In fact, as a college student, she had fallen in love with a Christian Japanese man. But her mother said, "To marry a Japanese means to surrender to the idols that the Japanese worship. The Japanese themselves might be Christians, but as long as Japan and the Japanese people are controlled by the idols, I don't believe it would be a good marriage."[189] Ei Sook had moved back to Korea alone, sad, but agreeing with her mother's wisdom.

As Ei Sook and Elder Park departed for Japan, Ei Sook says her mother was "content and beautiful and filled with the Holy Spirit."[190] Ei Sook strengthened herself with Queen Esther's words: "I will go in to the king, though it is against the law; and if I perish, I perish" (Esther 4:16). In Ei Sook's suitcase were the clothes her mother and sister had been saving for her wedding.

Now came the challenge of working as a team with Elder Park. Their faith expressed itself in quite different styles. Ei Sook felt that as much as possible they should work within the law. But Elder Park was sure laws would not stop them if they were following God. For example, he wouldn't try to get a passport, because he knew the authorities wouldn't give him one. But he also felt he didn't need one, because if God wanted them in Tokyo, no passport requirement would stand in God's way.

Ei Sook bought only a one-way train ticket to the coast, because she expected to be thrown into jail once they'd crossed over to Japan; so a return ticket would be wasted. But Elder Park laughed at even this purchase. "I don't need such a thing made by men since God is my refuge."[191] She didn't sit with him because she didn't want to be implicated when he got in trouble.

Near the coast, four harbor policemen boarded to check tickets. When she dared to look back, the policemen had already passed Elder

---

[188] Ibid., p. 60.
[189] Ibid., p. 167.
[190] Ibid., p. 65.
[191] Ibid.

Park's seat. He rose to join her, pushing past the policemen as he came. They didn't look toward him, only stepped aside. He reminded her that God was indeed his refuge.

Before they got on board the ship to Japan, she found Elder Park changing into his good clothes, and a policeman helping him. "Look, this policeman is kindly helping me. See, I must clothe myself like God's ambassador."[192] The policeman didn't seem even to hear him.

Boarding the boat, they were allowed to walk right past the policemen without showing passports. And so God did shelter them all the way to Tokyo—the team in which Elder Park was the feet and faith that could get them there, and Ei Sook was the voice that could speak the Japanese words.

## ADOPTION?

In Tokyo they had conversations with several important people, men they prayed would have influence with the authorities who could change conditions in Korea.

One was Major General Hibiki, the only surviving officer from the Russo-Japanese War. He was attending church when they found him. At the end of their time together, he asked a favor of her.

> "You are loved and used by God. Would you please become my adopted daughter? You could study at the seminary and work more for God."
>
> I did not know what to say to him. To become a daughter of this beloved Major General! How wonderful that would be! And to become a seminary student and study about the God I loved. It would have given me everything I had ever wanted or dreamed about from life. But at the same time I recalled the words that Satan had whispered to Jesus. "All these things will I give You, if You fall down and worship me" (Matthew 4:9, NASB).[193]

General Hibiki went on to try to persuade her to *live* for the Lord, rather than to *die* for him. That way she could stay in Japan and speak for God there.

---

[192] Ibid., p. 67.
[193] Ibid., pp. 83-84.

She grieved for the lonely old man, but answered, "You think I am a living person, but I am already dead. The moment I stood up for this task, I, Ahn Ei Sook, was dead and became a corpse. What can such a corpse do?"[194] They wept together.

Everyone with whom she and Elder Park talked was shocked at what they heard about conditions for Christians in Korea and sympathetic to their pleas. But it seemed, for various reasons, that none was any longer in a position to do anything about it.

## ARREST

Elder Park, though, had a final plan up his sleeve, or his pant leg, actually. He prepared a poster-roll of paper with these demands:

- The Japanese government should repent and withdraw its tyranny from Korea.
- Examine which is the true religion—Shintoism or Christianity.
- Burn a stack of wood and throw a Shinto believer and myself onto it. The one who is not burned shall prove the true religion.[195]

In March 1939, he smuggled the roll inside his pant leg into the gallery of the Imperial Diet, the Japanese legislature. At a crucial moment, he unfurled it and threw it down to the floor. "Jehovah's great commission," he shouted.[196] They were arrested.

## NEW KIND OF HOME

This was the beginning of six years of imprisonment for Ahn Ei Sook. She was sent back to Korea. At first the conditions were tolerable. In fact, to begin with she was under a sort of house arrest, living with her mother. But six years allowed plenty of time for changes in policy, for a succession of jails in different locations, and for things to move from bad to almost impossible.

To Ei Sook, it seemed as if prison were the home God had given her until it was time to die. She didn't put life on hold until death answered.

As she would have anywhere, she depended on God and his Word to sustain her. The Word that was at her disposal was the vast amount

---

194 Ibid., p. 84.
195 Ibid., p. 86.
196 Ibid., p. 89.

she had stored in the library of her heart. All the Scripture she had memorized was there to meditate on in prison as it had been at all other times in her life, for her to draw on to remember God's promises of faithfulness.

As she would have anywhere, she prayed for the people close to her. At one jail, she had lent the head jailer a Japanese Bible. Later he told her he was going to resign and go back to Japan. He wanted to start a new life because he'd come to hate his job. He said, "Officially, I am leaving for a rest, but a change has come into my heart. I want to live for a rewarding and true hope as you are doing." When she told him she had often prayed for him, he said, "You've prayed for me? Now I understand."[197]

As she would have anywhere, she sometimes was bold to speak her mind. One guard was extremely unpredictable and cruel. As soon as he was alone with the prisoners, he required something impossible— one particular night forcing them to sit up straight without moving all night long. Everyone waited for the blow to fall, when nobody-knew-what would set him into a rage. Finally, he chose a prisoner at random and lashed him with his belt until he was unconscious. The guard grinned and said, "That was good exercise." And he ordered another prisoner to clean up the bloody floor, beating him when he didn't work quickly enough.[198]

As Ei Sook lived through this hellish scene, she praised God for saving her from *eternal* hell. With paper and pen that had been permitted her, she wrote a twenty-page paper describing what she and fellow prisoners had seen and experienced. As a result, that guard was discharged, and the report was copied and sent to all the police departments in the country. For a while afterward, guards and policemen seemed more careful to keep the regulations.

Once she dared to interrupt the beating of one of the imprisoned pastors. She railed at the guard, "Go ahead! Beat me as much as you want, but leave him alone! . . . There is only love for God and for the people in his heart! How would you like to be beaten so ruthlessly when you get older? Go home and beat your father!"[199] The guard had nothing to say, like the lions whose mouths were shut against Daniel.[200]

[197] Ibid., pp. 116-117.
[198] Ibid., pp. 107-108.
[199] Ibid., pp. 124-125.
[200] Daniel 6:22.

In September of 1940, Ei Sook and other saints were transferred to the Pyongyang Prison. They were sure that this was a prelude to execution.

I couldn't help thinking what a day it was for Korean Christians. For a year the Japanese had starved and tortured the most loyal Korean Christian leaders in a ruthless attempt to stamp out their faith in Jesus Christ. Now those leaders, and myself among them, were to be executed. As one of the victims of the persecution, I would sing forever that I had been born and had lived for this purpose. . . .

I believed . . . that the churches of Christ would be built throughout the land. Hymns praising the Lord would be heard and proclaimed throughout the mountains, valleys, and towns. The few grains that were these believers' lives would fall into the earth, die, and bear much fruit.[201]

## BOTH THE SAME TO JESUS

But, as it turned out, it was not yet the appointed time for Ei Sook's death. Life stretched ahead in this new hellish home. One bitter winter night it was impossible to sleep because of the icy wind blowing through a crack in the floor. The women in the cell clustered tightly together for warmth. From another cell, they could hear the weird wailing and muttering of an insane young Chinese woman—a filthy woman whose hands were tied to keep her from hurting herself. She had been sentenced to death for killing her husband and hacking him into pieces

Ei Sook kept thinking of how Jesus would treat such a person. The other women were shocked when she asked them to pray that the woman could be moved to their cell. Ei Sook pestered the jailers until it was done.

All the other women huddled on the opposite side as far away as possible from the overwhelming stink. From behind, Ei Sook persistently held the woman's flailing body until they both fell exhausted to

---

the floor. When the woman fell asleep, Ei Sook held her excrement-crusted feet against her breast to warm them. The woman slept for three days without waking, Ei Sook holding her reeking feet and legs against her the whole time. When the woman woke, Ei Sook persuaded the guard to bring clean clothes. Then, by hand, she fed her the three days' worth of food—frozen in the icy cell—that she had saved for her. All the time, the woman cursed her.

Ei Sook knew that Jesus was fighting this battle too. Only his mercy could have held on to those legs and feet and could have loved a woman who hated so much.

Gradually, the woman began to listen when she heard, "I like you," spoken through Ei Sook's tears.

"Why do you like a person like me?" she asked.

"Because we are in the same situation." Ei Sook knew that they both needed Jesus equally, and that without him, both of them were destined for eternal hell.

One night the woman wept bitterly for her newborn son who had been taken from her when she was arrested. Afterward, Ei Sook spoke to her about her Creator who was calling her—her Creator who also can't forget his child.

A guard who returned after some time away could hardly believe this was the same woman who had been raving earlier.

One day to show her gratitude the woman gave Ei Sook the most valuable thing she had, her only possession, pieces of toilet paper hoarded from the daily small allotment. She asked Ei Sook to pray for her.

When the day of the woman's execution came, she left the cell serenely, saying, "Thank you very much."[202]

## DAY IN COURT

The Christians in Pyongyang prison had been held for varying lengths of time without trial. On a frigid January morning they were taken from their cells to go before the court. As Ei Sook stepped through the gates, she looked at the sky, long hidden from her in her cell. The few words she writes about that sight could be an Eastern poem that, in one thought, pictures a moment and a life.

---

[202] Ibid., pp. 171-180.

*I raised my eyes.*
*The sun was hidden behind the clouds.*
*Softly I prayed.*[203]

The prisoners' families waited for them outside the court building, welcoming them with a hymn: "God Is My Refuge and Strength." Ei Sook saw her mother—"She looked full of confidence."[204]

In an effort to silence the music, a jailer threw water on the people. It froze almost immediately, but that only raised the volume of their singing. Inside, the noise drowned out the judge's voice. Ei Sook asked if she could go outside to quiet them.

> He gave me permission and I dashed out. . . . "Now I must testify of the true God," I told them, "but the judge cannot hear me because of your singing. Would you please pray for me instead of singing?" . . .
>
> The great crowd bowed their heads and chorused, "Amen."[205]

As she stood before the amazed judge, he said, "You should be able to lead people in whatever way you wish. For what purpose have you been allured to ruin yourself, disorder society, and bring great loss to the nation?"[206]

This was the moment she'd waited months for—the moment to speak officially.

> "Mr. Judge, . . . what would you do if you saw someone drinking sewage water without knowing how filthy it was, and if he was telling others to drink it as well? . . . Whatever danger and disgrace might be brought upon me, I must . . . tell him not to drink the water. Jesus Christ, the Son of God in whom I have faith with all my might, died for such a purpose and has taught me to live accordingly. Therefore , . . I must testify of the truth and save the person who is drinking the sewage water."

[203] Ibid., p. 155.
[204] Ibid., p. 156.
[205] Ibid., p. 157.
[206] Ibid., p. 158.

"Who do you mean is drinking sewage water?" he demanded.

"Imperial Japan. The police force that is beating and killing the saints of God is drinking sewage water. For this reason I went to Tokyo and warned the important officials in the Japanese Diet. . . . Let me tell you how blind and crazy the Japanese government officials are. They trust the most malicious two-faced persons, promote them, honor them, and make them prosper in order to destroy the Christian Church and bring a curse upon the nation. . . . Japan is obviously rebelling against the true God. . . . God has called me, a Korean, to warn the Japanese government."[207]

She burst into tears, suddenly aware of the presence of God who had held the court silent so long to listen to her.

She was led out, and the other prisoners appeared one by one before the judge. As they all left the court, the crowd outside thundered a hymn: "All Hail the Power of Jesus' Name."

Re-entering the prison, she looked around at her fellow prisoners, knowing that for some the gates of this prison were as the gates of death and heaven. And when they were in heaven, "they would tell Jesus that it was because of his love and not because of their own powers that they had not denied their faith."[208]

## JUST AN APPLE, PLEASE

After several years of cold, illness, and starvation, her relatively young body was thin, bent, stooped, and shutting down. Even opening her eyes seemed too difficult. Suddenly she had a craving for apples. "Oh Jesus, I would like to eat an apple. You know my body system. You are the only One who can cure this painful desire. Please grant me one whole apple."[209]

She could think only of apples. Then she overheard jailers talking about a shipment of rotten apples that nobody would want. She begged for them, and they were delivered to her cell for her and the other women there. She ate and ate. The soggy brown apples seemed like

---

[207] Ibid., pp. 158-159.
[208] Ibid., p. 160.
[209] Ibid., p. 225.

heaven, like the fruit of heaven. The ache left her body, and all her body functions revived. And she praised God for sending apples that were *rotten*, because her teeth were too bad to eat fresh apples. She had been preparing herself for this joy back in those days when she was eating the worst rotten produce from the market.

## HER FATHER

In prison, she received word that her father had died. Near the end, he had wept for ten days for his sins, calling her name and her mother's, asking for forgiveness. And before he died, he called upon the name of Jesus and repented and praised God. For as long as she could remember, she had implored him to repent. Now her prayers were answered.[210]

## THE DEVOURING LION

The Shinto shrine caught up with Christians even in prison. It was decreed that on the eighth day of each month *every* person in Japanese-dominated countries was to bow at a shrine. Prisoners were not exempt. In their cells, they must bow in the direction of a great shrine. The chief jailer, knowing the "bad" influence that Ei Sook would be, moved all prisoners from her cell. Ei Sook fasted and prayed. Already physically depleted, the fear was almost enough to make her collapse and bow.

On the eighth day, she waited in dread for the signal. She described her faith as being like a small butterfly in a storm. She felt herself walking through the valley of the shadow of death.

The hour came. And passed. No signal! An hour later they found out that as the commandant stood to speak to the masses gathered at the shrine, he was interrupted for an urgent phone call. The governor's plane had been shot down by an American fighter plane, and so none of that governor's resolutions were being carried out.

She records her prayer. "Oh heavenly Father, you have shown me that you are the Savior. I was about to be devoured by the lion, but you saved me from its teeth. You are the living God. . . . I fear and love only you. I will listen to and obey you forever and ever."[211]

---

[210] Ibid., pp. 228-230.
[211] Ibid., p. 235.

## ALL KOREA A PRISON

There came a day when the prison doctor asked that she be released from prison because, without treatment, her eyes were going blind. Also her feet were frostbitten.

Her emotions swung wide between excitement over being with her mother and, on the other side, remembering the thanks and honor she had felt in the past at the prospect of being among the martyrs. She would lose this honor if she went home. She debated with herself all night but couldn't decide whether or not it was right to leave; so she left it in the Lord's hands.

The next morning, she was released to go home. She says, "I was so happy I wanted to sing aloud; yet a heavy uneasiness nudged me."[212]

She met her mother in the outer office. "Why are you coming out from here? Why should only you receive such a privilege? Other believers do not come out."[213] Ei Sook explained, "I'm not completely free. At home, good food in a warm room and plenty of rest will cure me. Then I will return to prison."[214]

The words her mother spoke then brought harsh reality to light. *All* Koreans were living in a prison, not just the ones behind bars.

> "Do you think you can get nutritious food these days? And where can you find a warm room? . . . We can get nothing except by rationing. Not even a grain of rice. . . . We have to eat bean husks, leeks, or anything we can get. Because of these, I am blind now; I can't see your face. . . . We can't get fuel. My feet are so frostbitten I can hardly walk. A citizen who is loyal to God has no place in this world. Christians in prison are dying, and so are the believers outside. . . .
>
> "Didn't you give everything to the Lord, including your eyes?"[215]

Ei Sook thanked her mother for opening her eyes to the reality that was beyond the stone prison walls. Then she asked the guard to let her return to her cell.

---

212 Ibid., p. 239.
213 Ibid.
214 Ibid., p. 240.
215 Ibid.

"I have never seen anything like this before," said the Korean senior officer. "The daughter is great. The mother is greater."[216]

Every evening from then on, Ei Sook looked out the small window to imagine her mother, stick-thin and frostbitten, on the other side of the great, red brick wall. She had told Ei Sook that she came every night to pray for her.

## FREEDOM

On August 15, 1945, Japan signed an unconditional surrender. World War II was over and Korea was free. The prisoners in and out of prison were elated. No more military draft . . . Hearing Korean spoken once again . . . Bearing one's own birth name again . . . And no more shrine worship. The shrines were all being burned.

Thirty-four Christians had entered Pyongyang prison in 1940. On August 17, 1945, when the cells were opened, there were fourteen who had survived. The jailer shouted to the people outside, "Ladies and gentlemen! These are the ones who for six long years refused to worship Japanese gods. They fought against severe torture, hunger, and cold, and have won out without bowing their heads to the idol worship of Japan. Today they are the champions of the faith!"[217]

The waiting crowd shouted, "Praise the name of Jesus!" and sang together:

> *All hail the power of Jesus' name!*
> *Let angels prostrate fall.*
> *Bring forth the royal diadem*
> *And crown him Lord of all.*[218]

The former prisoners were escorted into rickshaws and became part of a victorious, singing, shouting, praising parade through Pyongyang.

## AFTERWARD IN KOREA

The Japanese were leaving as unobtrusively and quickly as possible. And now, forty years after the Japanese had expelled them in 1904, the

---

[216] Ibid.

[217] Ibid., p. 257.

[218] James Ellor, "All Hail the Power of Jesus' Name."

Russians were back in North Korea, which had been separated from South Korea at the 38th parallel. Koreans who were old enough remembered the former Russian occupation as even worse than the Japanese. So large numbers were choosing to abandon their property and flee south rather than remain in Communist territory.

Ahn Ei Sook's family was forced to that decision after she was kidnapped by Communists who intended to transport her to Moscow and commandeer her to serve as a tool in their iron rule of Korea. Once again God miraculously gave her the opportunity simply to walk out and run away as she had once before.

With the help of several believers, she escaped and went to Seoul, in South Korea. There she met Kim Dong Myung, an engineer whom she described as "burning with God's love."[219] He became her husband. She had always wanted to marry an engineer. Her mother had always prayed that she'd marry a pastor. Ei Sook said, "Mother and I had competed against each other in our prayers. We both laughed at our predicament."[220] Later Ei Sook's husband gave up engineering to become a pastor.

## AFTERWARD IN AMERICA

Ei Sook's story had seeped out, and Americans wanted to hear more of it. American Christians paid for her to come to America to travel and give her testimony. She expected to return to Korea in three months.

But America became her new home. She and her husband Americanized their names to Don and Esther Ahn Kim. After earning a seminary degree, Don became the founding pastor of the Berendo Street Baptist Church in Los Angeles. This was only the second Korean congregation of the Southern Baptists in the USA. Their apartment served as an unofficial drop-in center and hostel for dozens of young people who needed a home away from home and a Christian foundation.

During their years at Berendo Street, they also returned repeatedly to Korea, working at church planting there as well as in America. Esther traveled around the world, speaking of God's faithfulness and power.

Until her death, when she was in her nineties, she was still admonishing people and praying for them. And she was still memorizing

---

[219] Kim, p. 275.
[220] Ibid., p. 175.

Scripture, now in English, to add to her heart library of Korean and Japanese.

The first public crisis of Ei Sook's life was the day she was expected to bow at Namsan Mountain. When I think about her inner experiences during those hours, I realize there's a similar pattern woven through her subsequent years. And we often trace that same pattern within ourselves when we are afraid.

1. She *remembers an example* of someone in a similar situation—in this case, Shadrach, Meshach, and Abednego in the fire.

2. The effect is that their confidence in God gives her *confidence*: "With God's help, I will never bow."

3. She *prays*.

4. In response, God fills her with *peace*.

5. The peace leads her to *commitment* broader than just for this particular event: "I am not going to live my youthful life for myself. I will offer it to the Lord."

6. She *remembers a promise* from God: "No one can snatch my sheep from my hand."

7. *Fear* falls on her again as the moment draws near. One prayer and one promise is not enough to ward off fear permanently.

8. She *confesses* her weakness and fear to God.

9. He reminds her again of his *promise*: "I know my sheep and they follow me." We need God's promises over and over. The bigger our fear, the more often we need God's assurance.

10. She *acts*. She follows through with her confident intention to remain standing.

11. But that's not the end. *Uncertainty* comes again. "What if I can't stand the consequences?"

12. Once again, she finds comfort from God's Word, his *promise:* "I will not leave you desolate. . . . My peace I give you."

This kind of fluctuation is so familiar to us. We are afraid. We pray. God gives us confidence. But we don't stay confident. We fall again into fear. And again he rescues us, giving us courage to carry through with the fearful thing that awaits us. In fact, this *is* the pattern of life. We simply experience it more intensely in hours of crisis.

Throughout her story, the pendulum in Ei Sook's life sweeps wide, from cowering fear and almost giving up on one side, to bold, fearless words and acts on the other side, when the moment for them arrives.

We mustn't overlook the amazing weapon she wielded in this battle for faith, the amount of Scripture she obviously already had memorized. She didn't need the time or resources to hunt up a concordance or Bible to find an appropriate word from God. The Word was on the tip of her tongue exactly when she needed to preach to herself and when she needed to hear God speaking.

Memorized Scripture played an essential part in the next stage of Ei Sook's life—preparation for suffering. I think if Ahn Ei Sook were here, she would tell us that it is good to prepare for whatever lies ahead of us, whether it's persecution and martyrdom or something less drastic. She would probably start by helping us see that suffering is normal:

> I always felt strengthened when I talked with Mother about God and His love. I began to think that life might be worth living in this time of persecution. It might even be a truer picture of the believer to agonize, to suffer, to be hated, and tortured, and even to be killed in obeying God's words rather than to live an ordinary, uneventful life.[221]

Some of her preparatory measures should be standard fare for us, whatever our current situation.
- Prayer
- Worship
- Practicing living simply
- Generosity with good things, not just leftovers
- Memorizing Scripture
- Listening to people's stories about trouble and God

Perhaps she would want to leave us with these words from God about suffering and persecution:

> *Blessed are you when others revile you and persecute you and utter all kinds of evil against you falsely on my account. Rejoice and be glad, for your reward is great in heaven, for so they persecuted the prophets who were before you.*
> MATTHEW 5:11-12

---

[221] Ibid., pp. 27-28.

*Everyone who acknowledges me before men, the Son of Man also
will acknowledge before the angels of God.*

LUKE 12:8

*Rejoice insofar as you share Christ's sufferings, that you may also
rejoice and be glad when his glory is revealed. If you are insulted
for the name of Christ, you are blessed, because the Spirit of glory
and of God rests upon you.*

1 PETER 4:13-14

*But [God] said to me, "My grace is sufficient for you, for my
power is made perfect in weakness."*

2 CORINTHIANS 12:9

*I consider that the sufferings of this present time are not worth
comparing with the glory that is to be revealed to us.*

ROMANS 8:18

*Who shall separate us from the love of Christ? Shall tribulation,
or distress, or persecution, or famine, or nakedness, or danger, or
sword? As it is written, "For your sake we are being killed all the
day long; we are regarded as sheep to be slaughtered." No, in all
these things we are more than conquerors through him who loved
us. For I am sure that neither death nor life, nor angels nor rulers,
nor things present nor things to come, nor powers, nor height nor
depth, nor anything else in all creation, will be able to separate
us from the love of God in Christ Jesus our Lord.*

ROMANS 8:35-39

She might also add the words from one of the many hymns she
knew by heart:

> *Let goods and kindred go, this mortal life also,*
> *The body they may kill, God's truth abideth still,*
> *His kingdom is forever.*[222]

When God calls us to suffer, he is offering us the privilege of
understanding more clearly the incarnation of Christ. Experiencing

---

[222] Martin Luther, "A Mighty Fortress Is Our God."

Christmas in prison offered Ei Sook a glimpse of the contrast it must have been for Jesus, coming from the heavenly places into this world.

Christmas had come in the prison. It arrived amid the pathetic starvation and severe coldness and the heartbreaking torture by the most vulgar jailers. Christmas was indeed a joyous occasion. How I had sung praises to God on other Christmases and rejoiced with holiness pouring into my heart. But now I was being touched by a truth that I never before had known. God had truly sent His only Son into this dark and filthy world. He humbled Himself to be born as a man. He experienced poverty, weariness, sorrow, pain, and great persecution. He was hated and rejected, hit and spat upon, and was hung on the cross to die! And His death was for the purpose of saving such a sinful and worthless person as myself.[223]

At another time, a young cellmate was crippled by fear. As Ei Sook comforted her, she herself saw Jesus more clearly.

Every time we heard a jailer coming, she thought the time had arrived for her to be taken out to be executed. "Try not to worry about it," I told her. "I may be executed with you. Why don't we live together as close friends and die together?"

She seemed to be greatly comforted by what I had told her, and at last she was able to approach me without any reservation. I found that being the same kind of person had a special effect on her. That was what Jesus had done for us. He became a human being like ourselves and walked among us. If He had not become a man, He would not have been able to save us.[224]

Ei Sook's suffering holds another lesson for us. When suffering is great, we are vulnerable to doubt. She wrote about one particular period of agonizing torture:

I pleaded with Him to take away my senses and to let me die. Surely if I had been a strong Christian a miracle would have

223 Kim, p. 169.
224 Ibid., p. 211-212.

occurred to take away the pain, or I would have been given the strength to bear it calmly. In my desperate prayer I was complaining. Realizing my weakness, I became afraid. I thought I had faith, but did I really have it or was I just deceiving myself? Would Jesus forsake such a sinful person? Was I a valueless, sinful child, of no concern to God? I was confused. Because of the excruciating pain, I could not recite any Scripture.[225]

That last sentence holds the key to her slide into despair. In those moments she didn't have God's Word—no sword to wield against the fiery darts of the evil one. She was able, though, to utter a weak prayer, and God proved himself to be near.

As we look at the strength of God displayed in the life of Ahn Ei Sook, we must also take lessons from her mother. I pray that all of us who are mothers and mentors (whether officially or simply by virtue of having slightly more experience) will manage the balance that Ei Sook's mother did. She was gentle to her sickly daughter, and she fostered her childhood faith into adulthood. But that nurturing spirit was rounded out by her love for truth and her frankness in speaking it. She was not overwhelmed with fear when her daughter was in a frightening situation. Sympathy did not make her soft. She must have shed many tears on Ei Sook's behalf. But her tears and fears seem to have been reserved for private moments between her and God.

I don't mean that we should be stoic stones. I do mean that fear and illness need to be met with courage and strength, not with the sort of sympathy that escalates the sense of helplessness.

Ei Sook's mother provides us with a model in a different setting as well—the setting where she herself is the one who is suffering, suffering the loss of her child. As Ei Sook left for Japan, expecting to be arrested and executed, she said her mother was "content and beautiful and filled with the Holy Spirit."[226] What a model for us in sending our children and friends where God leads them.

---

[225] Ibid., p. 219.
[226] Ibid., p. 65.

∽∽∽

The town of Bhak Chon, the birthplace of Ahn Ei Sook, lay beside the crystal-clear Tarung River. Towering over the town was Won Su Bong Mountain. Because both the mountain and the river were so stunningly beautiful, the people in town often had said a hero would be born there.

∽∽∽

*As I became acquainted with Esther Ahn Kim and this story of Christianity in Korea, I often thought about my friends of Korean background in America, wondering how their lives and their families' lives had been touched by that history. And so this story of Esther Ahn Kim in Korea is dedicated to those friends, especially to Sam and Shua Shin who first gave me reason to turn my eyes toward Korea . . . to John and Sung Kim, whose passion is to awaken hearts to Jesus . . . and to Charles Park, who has been like a son at our table.*

$B$ut whatever gain I had, I counted as loss for the sake of Christ.
Indeed, I count everything as loss because of
the surpassing worth of knowing Christ Jesus my Lord.
For his sake I have suffered the loss of all things and
count them as rubbish, in order that I may gain Christ
and be found in him, not having a righteousness of my
own that comes from the law, but that which comes
through faith in Christ, the righteousness from God that
depends on faith—that I may know him and the power of
his resurrection, and may share his sufferings,
becoming like him in his death, that by any means possible
I may attain the resurrection from the dead.

PHILIPPIANS 3:7-11

# HELEN ROSEVEARE
*Faithful in Loss*

⟨∞⟩

In 1482, ten years before Columbus launched out for the western edge of the great sea, Diogo Cão sailed south from Lisbon, the latest in a celebrated line of Portuguese adventurers. Cautiously hugging the coast aport, each explorer dreamed of pressing farther south into the unknown than anyone had before. So when Cão rounded the western hump of the African continent and found his ship in a tide of muddy, yellowish *fresh* water, he became the first European to ride the surge of the mighty Congo River pouring its 1.5 million cubic feet of water per second into the Atlantic Ocean.

One of the names of the river is Nzere, "the river that swallows all rivers." It also swallowed outsiders who tried to follow its turbulent course through the tightly tangled, malarial jungle and past the lairs of secluded, suspicious peoples. After Cão's discovery of the river, nearly 400 years passed until a European, Henry Morton Stanley, completed the journey of the entire length of the Congo River in 1877, traveling by canoe from the interior to the Atlantic. He had become famous a few years earlier after his successful search for the missionary-explorer the waiting world had lost touch with—"Dr. Livingstone, I presume!"

Stanley's traverse of the Congo awakened European and American interest in that hidden giant. The very next year, Protestant missionaries began to arrive in Congo.[227] But the river and the surrounding miles of nearly impenetrable rainforest were by no means wide open to the public. The area still remained mysterious and hard to reach in 1925, when Helen Roseveare was born in Haileybury, England, only twenty-seven years after Stanley's river expedition and eleven years after his death.

Helen's family lived in a country whose citizens were at least

---

[227] http://www.pcusa.org/pcusa/wmd/ep/country/demreli.htm, accessed 2/18/05.

somewhat aware of the nations and peoples with whom Britain had a colonial relationship. This seems to have been particularly true in the Roseveare household. Helen was not the only one of them who later ended up in Africa. Helen's brother Robert taught for more than a decade in various places in southern Africa.[228] Their father, Sir Martin Roseveare, moved to Malawi at the age of fifty-nine and "set up the educational system in Malawi, where he lived until his death,"[229] at eighty-six.

Helen also recalls her Sunday school teacher talking about faraway places and people:

> I vividly remember that wonderful day (my eighth birthday) when she talked to us of India, and we cut out pictures of Indian children and stuck them in our "Missionary Prayer Book." It was then that the quiet resolve was made. When I grow up, I will go to tell other boys and girls about the Lord Jesus—a child's determination that never faded.[230]

Helen loved the "air of mystery [that] laid the foundation of Sundays." Attending their Anglo-Catholic church,[231] she was stirred by

> The cool, dim building, with high, carved wood pews . . . the choir boys in surplice and ruff . . . the cross and incense . . . the pealing organ and rich strange music that filled the building right up to the great carved dome . . . the sermon with its grave cadences; all these I loved, absorbing almost unconsciously a lasting impression of beauty and solemnity.[232]

But the place of church in the family's life was overshadowed by their scholarly achievements, especially in mathematically related fields. From early childhood, Helen bore the weight of "the absorbing necessity of being loved and wanted"[233]—of being good enough. As

---

[228] http://www.timesonline.co.uk/article/0,,60-1428343_1,00.html. Obituary of Robert Roseveare, posted 1/07/05. Accessed 2/18/05.

[229] Personal correspondence from Helen Roseveare, February 19, 2005.

[230] Helen Roseveare, *Give Me This Mountain: An Autobiography* (London: Inter-Varsity Fellowship, 1966), p. 15.

[231] An Anglican parish (Church of England) that leans heavily toward the belief and liturgy of Roman Catholicism.

[232] Roseveare, *Give Me This Mountain*, pp. 14-15.

[233] Ibid., p. 15.

she grew, this developed into the drive to excel in school—and not just to excel, but to be number one. She "felt, deep down, that if I didn't do well I would fail to win the love and respect of my parents and brother, always so deeply important to me."[234] As a result, she seldom did fail. The child Helen was already plagued by the very doubts, insecurity, and pride that would be the core of most of her recurring spiritual struggles as an adult.

> Somehow in the midst of this, I became conscious of God. . . .
> I needed Someone who was so big he could be bigger than me!
> And so God came in—and I was confirmed [with the other 12-year-olds]. . . . I'm sure I didn't understand the real meaning or full significance of it. . . . In a stumbling way, it was the conscious start of my search for Him. . . . God knew—and accepted—and leant towards me to draw me steadily nearer Himself.[235]

Throughout her secondary school years, her hunger for God expressed itself in earnest efforts "to help others, to be kindly, to be sincere."[236] These efforts drove her more deeply into perfectionism. She was "stretching out after the Unseen Power who could meet all needs. And yet . . . the needs were getting bigger; the hopelessness was more hopeless; the futility of life itself at times became almost unbearable. . . . And all the while God was driving me to see that in myself there was nothing, absolutely nothing of any worth. . . . How could I find him . . . and lose myself in him?"[237]

In July 1944, Helen began studying medicine as a student in Newnham College of Cambridge University. Awash with shyness and the fear of inferiority, she was taken under the wings of some young women whose "lives and faces radiated a happiness and peace that was very nearly infectious, and quite obviously satisfying."[238] They were members of the Cambridge Inter-Collegiate Christian Union, and Helen began to attend Bible studies, Christian lectures, and other activities with them.

---

234 Ibid., p. 18.
235 Ibid., p. 18.
236 Ibid., p. 22.
237 Ibid., pp. 22-23.
238 Ibid., p. 29.

Even now I can remember the first time I sang, "More about Jesus would I know. . . ." My whole being was deeply stirred. We were sitting round the fire in Sylvia's room for a Bible study one evening late in October. I don't remember the study—the words of the hymn kept repeating in my mind. When the others dispersed, I stayed sitting on the rug, gazing into the fire, with a great longing stirring in my innermost soul. "More about Jesus would I know. . . ." It was as though a window opened and slowly, amazedly, in stunned awe, I glimpsed through—a twig sputtered on the fire, and it was lost. Again, urgently, holding on to the moment, willing the very presence of Jesus to become real to my soul, the glory seemed to shine, a light of great brightness. I hardly dared to breathe; it felt as though life was suspended, caught up, breathless. My heart filled with joy and wonder—and it passed.[239]

Helen began to read the Scriptures avidly. Her friends believed her to be converted, but she says, "As yet I had no peace, no heart satisfaction. . . . I was sure it was real and the truth; but I was also conscious that I lacked something."[240]

During Christmas break in 1945, Helen's younger sister had mumps, so Helen couldn't go home. Her friends arranged for her to attend a house party that was a training session for Christian workers. In preparation for one class, she pored over the book of Romans and became so immersed that she unwittingly stayed up all night. Then the next day, from those heights she plummeted because of an argument with someone at the supper table.

I . . . rushed upstairs, bitterly ashamed of having been drawn into the argument and losing control of myself. Suddenly, I flung myself on my bed, in a flood of tears and loneliness. With an overwhelming sense of failure and helplessness I cried out to God (if there was a God) to meet with me and to make utterly real and vital to me *Himself*. I raised my eyes, and through my tears read a text on the wall: "Be still, and know that I am God" (Psalm 46:10). That was all. Immediately the

---

[239] Ibid., pp. 30-31.
[240] Ibid., p. 31.

whole burden fell away in a moment. Be still and know God, whose name is "I am." . . . Stop striving to understand with the intellect. Just be still, and know him. In that moment, a great flood of peace and joy and unutterable happiness flooded in, and I *knew* that He and I had entered into a new relationship.[241]

She also knew that this hadn't come from out of the blue. God had been preparing her and had used her searching to help her find him.

The steady reading of Scripture in the previous months, the careful listening to doctrinal teaching both at the houseparty and in Christian Union meetings, had prepared the way. For years the Holy Spirit had been opening my eyes to a sense of sin, convicting me of my unworthiness before a Holy God. But now came the wonderful gift of repentance. God poured out His grace in forgiveness, in cleansing from all the uncleanness of sin, and in revealing, at this time, the amazing wonder of the friendship of Christ.[242]

And God was not yet done working. When Helen rejoined the group and told them what had happened, a veteran Bible teacher wrote Philippians 3:10 in her new Bible: "That I may know him, and the power of his resurrection, and the fellowship of his sufferings, being made conformable unto his death" (KJV).

He said to me, "Tonight you've entered into the first part of the verse, 'That I may know him.'" This is only the beginning, and there's a long journey ahead. My prayer for you is that you will go on through the verse to know "the power of his resurrection" and also, God willing, one day perhaps, "the fellowship of his sufferings, being made conformable unto his death."[243]

Helen went back to her room that night to read the verse in its context. And so, on the very day that God drew her to himself, he also showed her his words that twenty years later would give meaning to the most painful, seemingly irrational event in her whole life.

---

[241] Ibid., p. 35.
[242] Ibid., pp. 35-36.
[243] Ibid., p. 36-37.

## But Whatever Gain I Had, I Counted as Loss for the Sake of Christ

Even before she had become a Christian, Helen knew she was called to missions. She felt this call so strongly that it was difficult for her to understand why every Christian wasn't preparing for missions. Alongside her medical training, she accepted opportunities to be a summer camp doctor, to lead Bible studies, to give her testimony in public. Above all, she delved into the Scripture to fill vast gaps in her knowledge and to know God more intimately.

Parallel with her growing ministry and heavier hours of professional training was a nagging sense of doubt and insecurity.

> I tended to call certain sins weaknesses—or human frailties—and thereby to excuse them. It was nicer to speak of exaggeration . . . than to speak of lying. Yet I felt I was practising mental dishonesty in making such excuses for myself. . . . Then slowly there dawned a sense of exhaustion. The joy and excitement of the first three years suddenly seemed to drain away. . . . Work began to get on top of me; unhappiness, loneliness, fear, inferiority, all began to be acutely present. At the same time Bible study and prayer became perfunctory instead of joyous. . . . Witness continued, but with no real faith or expectation of seeing results. Looking back it is easy to realize that at least part of the explanation lies in the fact that, like many of my fellow medical students, I was suffering from overwork and strain resulting from a very full programme. . . . I . . . thought this exhaustion meant spiritual failure.[244]

Her doubts affected her professional work as well.

> In the wards and in front of other doctors I was very conscious of inferiority, or rather a fear of what others thought. This crippling shyness just had to be subdued and overcome by a daily dying to self, by a vigorous painful effort. Yet there was little success.[245]

---

[244] Ibid., pp. 56-57.
[245] Ibid., p. 60.

Years later, she wrote that she had misunderstood in those early years what it meant to grow in the Christian life. She had thought it should be a constant climb, achieving ever greater heights until one finally reached the mountain's peak. At that later time, with the perspective of years and maturity, she knew that life is not just one peak, but a range, with valleys between the mountains.

> I found frequently that I climbed in glorious sunshine . . . my face set determinedly for the nearest peak I could see. As I reached it, I revelled in the sense of achievement and victory and in the glorious view. . . . Then, slowly, my imagination would be caught by the next peak ahead . . . and eventually the resolve would form to set off upwards again. . . .
>
> As I went down from the present peak into the valley between the mountains, I was often shadowed by the very peak I had been enjoying. This I interpreted in a sense of failure and this often led to despair. . . . I see now that I was wrong. . . . The going down was merely an initial moving forward towards the next higher ground, never a going back to base level, so to speak. The shadow was only relative after the brightness of the sun; the valley could provide a period of rest for working out the experiences previously learnt, a time for refreshment preparatory for the next hard climb. Had I understood this meaning of the sunshine and shadow in my life rather than interpreting my various experiences along life's way as "up" and "down," I might have saved myself many deep heartaches.[246]

In the last year of her medical preparation, she lost her voice, which provided an occasion for God to display his power and purpose. After surgery to remove benign nodes from her vocal cords, she was not allowed to speak for a few days. One morning, in the stillness of her hospital room, she experienced the light-giving presence of God— invisible, but as if she could almost see him.

> From that morning, a hatred of sin was born. Till then I had hated the consequence of sin, the shame of failure, the fear of

---

[246] Ibid., p. 10.

exposure. . . . Suddenly I now knew an intense hatred of all that had crucified my Lord. It was the turning-point for me. The downward path from the peak of happiness, with its puzzlements and questionings, was arrested. Suddenly the next peak stood out clearly ahead. . . . He who was calling me on to service overseas was standing there, gently smiling, promising His presence and companionship and enabling, telling me to look forward and upward, not backward or inward. Suddenly the months of struggle and longing were over; I was satisfied. Not that my doubts were exactly explained; they no longer seemed to need explanation.[247]

This assurance took a blow when the time came to try out her voice, and she could only bark like a dog or whisper hoarsely. What would this mean for her medical career and missions?

Slowly another voice began to force itself through the night into my heart. "Can you not trust Me?" it seemed to whisper. . . . "Have you not used your voice for your own ends, for your own glorification for years? I will give you a new voice for use in My service."[248]

She was released from the hospital on Good Friday. That Easter evening she and some old friends heard a sermon about letting the Holy Spirit take possession of their lives and fill them with God's holiness. When the friends questioned whether this was possible, Helen answered clearly a ringing, "Yes!" God had healed her voice.

After the end of medical school, Helen spent time in candidate training at the WEC (Worldwide Evangelization Crusade). Then there were eight months of learning French in Brussels and studying tropical diseases in Antwerp. Also during these months she suffered a dog bite, jaundice, and mumps. After this, three months were filled with raising financial and prayer support, shopping for personal and medical supplies, packing, acquiring visas and inoculations, and completing other preparation for traveling and getting settled thousands of miles from home.

---

[247] Ibid., p, 64.
[248] Ibid., p. 65.

Saturday, February 14, 1953, she sailed from London, traveling through the straits of Gibraltar, along the length of the Mediterranean, through the Suez Canal, and on to Mombasa, Kenya, on Africa's eastern coast. Aboard the train to Nairobi, this twenty-seven-year-old woman was eager as a child:

> Excitement? I couldn't eat or talk. I was barely able to think for it! I rushed from side to side of the compartment so as not to miss anything. At each station on the long slow climb up from sea-level to 5,000 feet I leapt down, to stand on African soil, to read the name of the station and its height, to sense the *feeling* of Africa, its smells, and ways, and moods.[249]

Staying with missionaries along the way, Helen traveled by trains and lake steamers and truck halfway across Africa to her new home, arriving on Tuesday evening, March 17, 1953, six weeks after she had left London. Her assignment was to establish medical services and training in the remote village of Ibambi in the northeastern part of the Belgian Congo.[250]

This is not how most newly minted British physicians would have chosen to profit from their years of training.

## I COUNT EVERYTHING AS LOSS BECAUSE OF THE SURPASSING WORTH OF KNOWING CHRIST JESUS MY LORD

She and her fellow travelers—returning missionaries—entered Ibambi through a floral arch, surrounded by an excited crowd.

> Then Pasteur Ndugu, senior elder of the African church, stepped forward to welcome us all, and myself in particular as the "new" missionary, in the name of the church. "We, the church of Jesus Christ in Congo, and we, her elders, welcome

---

[249] Ibid., p. 76.

[250] Though this country has worn a series of names through history, it is often known familiarly simply as Congo. In ancient days, the area was part of the Kingdom of Kongo and eventually was known as Congo. It was renamed Congo Free State in 1895 when the king of Belgium, acting independently, persuaded other European leaders to recognize him as king of Congo. When the Belgian government took over in 1908, it became Belgian Congo. Upon gaining independence in 1960, the country became Congo. In 1971, the national government renamed the country Zaire. Following an internal rebellion, the current name was adopted in 1997, Democratic Republic of the Congo. A neighboring but separate nation is Republic of Congo, familiarly known as Congo Brazzaville.

you, our child, into our midst." I never forgot that moment or those words. What a privilege for a young missionary to be "their child," one of them, to be cared for, nurtured, loved and taught by them.[251]

Over the years and in various books, Helen told several stories of Pastor Ndugu's impact on her life. And beginning this very first day in Ibambi, the pastor's wife enfolded Helen with a love that surprised her and melted her reserved nature.

My tears overflowed in the infinite sense of joy that filled my heart. They surged around us, shaking our hands a hundred times, chatting and laughing . . . and slowly I slipped to the back of the veranda, leaning against the wall, emotionally overwhelmed. . . .

Suddenly, quietly, there was dear Tamoma . . . her gentle eyes looking deeply into mine. . . . "Ninakupenda," she said—"I love you"—and hugged me! . . . She'd never met me before. . . . But she loved me!

She had prayed for years that God would send a doctor. . . . When she had heard that a student doctor was interested, she had redoubled her prayers for God . . . [to] give her success in her exams. . . . When . . . the exams were at last safely over, and the young lady doctor was in the Mission's headquarters being prepared for future service, Tamoma prayed on that there would be no proverbial "slip between the call and the ship." . . .

And I had at last arrived. And she loved me!

From that moment, Tamoma and [her pastor husband] Ndugu took me into their hearts . . . as their own child. . . . It was my first introduction to a Christian family who obeyed literally Christ's command to His disciples: "Love one another," that thereby "all men will know that you are My disciples" (John 13:35).

That a senior woman of different culture and a different language . . . was willing to offer me Christ's love without first "getting to know" me, to evaluate whether I was worth loving or not, was a quite extraordinary experience. Nothing else in

---

251 Roseveare, *Give Me This Mountain*, p. 78.

my first month honestly caused me culture shock, but this one act—a warmhearted hug . . . a gentle comment: "I love you"—*this* caused me a lot of personal heart searching. Would I have loved Tamoma with the same unquestioning warmth if our situations had been reversed? Was it merely a matter of the proverbial British reserve . . . or was it really something much more fundamental, a lack of holy Christlikeness on my part?

"But God demonstrates His own love for us in this: While we were still sinners, Christ died for us"(Romans 5:8).

Christ loved me enough to die for me while I was yet His enemy. If God had waited for me to learn to love Him before He died, I would never have been saved. I knew that with my head, but when I met someone who behaved in such a completely Christlike way, I was amazed.[252]

Later in her life, someone indeed suggested to Helen that God sent her to Africa because there were things she couldn't learn about him in England—like grasping the Christlike kind of love that Tamoma showed her. Some other adjustments were easier.

Adapting to culture and new dietary regimes was honestly little of a problem to me. I was so excited to be there and wanted to become one with the people as fast as I could, that I noticed no barrier or sense of shock. Maybe our fairly rigourous upbringing during the rationing shortages of Word War II, and having spent most of childhood's holidays camping or mountaineering, was a real help in developing an adaptability to any circumstances. And I was so thrilled to have arrived in Africa, I would have enjoyed practically anything.[253]

## FOR HIS SAKE I HAVE SUFFERED THE LOSS OF ALL THINGS

Helen's professional adjustment in this remote, undeveloped area was much harder than her adjustment to the diet. She discovered immediately that she must set aside the medical standards that had been drilled into her for years, particularly the importance of practicing only the

---

[252] Helen Roseveare, *Living Holiness* (Minneapolis: Bethany House Publishers, 1986), pp. 82-84.
[253] Helen Roseveare, *Living Sacrifice* (Minneapolis: Bethany House Publishers, 1979), p. 28.

best medicine possible. She didn't want to make guinea pigs of her patients while she learned how to work in this new place.

> Starting with nothing but an upturned tea-chest, a camp table and a stool, a primus stove and saucepan, I discovered what it was to be fenced in with difficulties. . . . So much that should have been done to maintain medical standards just proved impossible. Good training told me that a patient with a high fever and chills, painful eyes and profuse sweating was probably suffering from malaria. Treatment . . . was quinine in a suitable dose according to the weight of the patient, but only after the diagnosis had been confirmed in the laboratory. . . . This microscopic procedure . . . would take a well-trained technician at least 5 minutes. With fifty or more patients daily showing symptoms of malaria, this would have added over four hours to the day's work. With no electricity, these four hours would have to be . . . during daylight. Yet besides these fifty malarial patients, there were probably [150 others with other complaints]. . . .
>
> The day simply wasn't long enough. And so malarial symptoms prompted treatment with quinine, with a quick estimate of weight and no laboratory confirmation. . . .
>
> When I began to realize that over 200 patients were being treated daily . . . and 75% or more were responding immediately to the initial treatment given, I began to see that it was not necessarily a lowering of standards to treat malarial symptoms without laboratory confirmation: rather it was a necessary adaptation to circumstances. . . . These same 200 patients daily, having received something that aided their physical pain to subside, were then much more open to listen to the preaching of the gospel.[254]

## I COUNT THEM AS RUBBISH, IN ORDER THAT I MAY GAIN CHRIST AND BE FOUND IN HIM

Helen was also assigned to begin a training program for medical workers. The first students began arriving to learn nursing. Their ages

---

[254] Helen Roseveare, *He Gave Us a Valley* (Downers Grove, Ill.: InterVarsity Press, 1976), pp. 14-15.

ranged from about eighteen to twenty-four, and their educational background was the equivalent of about grades five through seven.[255] Among the first class of students was John Mangadima, who would grow to be a friend and colleague throughout Helen's years in Congo.

Helen was not trained as a teacher or a nurse. There was no ready-made curriculum. And all the teaching was in French and Swahili. Neither of these languages was the native tongue of Helen or any of the students.

> God taught me to teach as the need arose. . . . A patient came in with burning fever, and so we launched into a lecture on how to use, read and understand a thermometer. . . . A baby was brought in with broncho-pneumonia, and I demonstrated the use of the stethoscope and how to arrive at a diagnosis. An endless stream of patients, with a seemingly limitless supply of abdominal symptoms, provided us with material to discover the use of the microscope and to learn to recognize every possible species of parasite.[256]

Serving as mentor to the nursing students meant taking additional time for each medical procedure. This had to fit into days that already were too short.

> The work-load and consequent inability to take a night off-duty, or to go away for a weekend, brought out in me an irritability and shortness of temper that often caused me considerable loss of sleep. I'd always had a hasty temper, but this had largely been under control . . . since my conversion to Christ. Now the hot and angry word would burst out again, before I could control it, and to my shame. Patients who came to the dining room window while we were at the midday meal would get a sharp word from me to "go to the dispensary, and not bring your germs to our home"—and a sad look would come to the faces of senior missionaries, who treated every visitor to their home with kindliness and respect.
>
> Evangelist Danga . . . took me to task for this un-Christlike

---

[255] Personal correspondence from Helen Roseveare, February 19, 2005.
[256] Roseveare, *He Gave Us a Valley*, pp. 15-16.

behavior. "Don't excuse yourself. Call sin sin and temper temper. Then face up to the fact that your white skin makes you no different from the rest of us. You need His cleansing and forgiveness, His infilling and indwelling, the same as we do. If you can only show us Doctor Helen, you might as well as go home: the people need to see Jesus."[257]

After eighteen months at Ibambi, Helen was moved in 1955 by her mission board to Nebobongo, because she was needed to take over the medical work there. So the nursing students and training program moved with Helen to Nebobongo, seven miles from Ibambi.

## NOT HAVING A RIGHTEOUSNESS OF MY OWN THAT COMES FROM THE LAW, BUT THAT WHICH COMES THROUGH FAITH IN CHRIST, THE RIGHTEOUSNESS FROM GOD THAT DEPENDS ON FAITH

She would remain in Nebobongo for ten years, overseeing the existing leprosy-care center and children's home and establishing forty-eight rural health clinics in the immediate vicinity, a training center for paramedical workers, and a 100-bed hospital and maternity service. The hospital and training college literally had to be built from the ground up, and the only people to do it were Helen and her European colleague Florence Stebbing and the students.

> We learned to make bricks. . . . We learned the intricacies of brick kilns . . . how a spirit level works, and the right mixture of cement and sand for concrete . . . how to saw planks from a felled tree . . . how to measure and raise these planks as triangular roof trusses, to carry the corrugated asbestos sheeting. . . .[258]

When the task seemed too big for them, God provided unexpected solutions. For instance, one set of trusses was dangerously heavy and unwieldy for the students and Helen, roofing novices, to manage. They prayed for an experienced roofer. About that time, a missionary was

---

[257] Ibid., pp. 16-17.
[258] Roseveare, *Living Sacrifice,* p. 40.

brought to wait through her at-risk pregnancy. Out of the blue, Helen asked the husband, "Are you a roofer?" He was.

Construction was not the only challenge. Every necessity offered its own difficulties.

> We learned auto mechanics . . . from sheer necessity. . . . We needed the vehicle to act as an ambulance . . . as a builder's truck . . . as a food van. . . . The only way to do repairs was for me to get underneath or inside with an African colleague, and by trial and error, experiment till we succeeded.
>
> We learned Swahili and French, and a smattering of Bangala and Kibudu; and then tackled the task of expressing medical truths without scientific jargon. . . . We wrote our first textbook in Swahili. . . . Stencils were made, and eventually one hundred copies were duplicated on an old-fashioned machine where each page was meticulously rubbed off individually and laid out to dry. Agonized stories could be told of days when wind crept in through the shutters and lifted the pages in an avalanche of disaster![259]

Writing textbooks could have been a full-time job. So could construction of a hospital and medical training school. And the medical demands were, in themselves, more than full time. Helen couldn't forget that she had felt called to *medical* missions, but the various other roles kept pushing in, competing for priority in the limited hours of a day.

One morning for example, she was at the brick kiln, her hands scratched and rough from the work, when she was called to the hospital to perform an emergency surgery.

> I began to scrub up: my hands smarted under the bristles. I held out my hands to the nurse to pour on antiseptic alcohol: I drew up my breath sharply at the stinging pain. And in my mind, a small voice of complaint started.
>
> Why had God not arranged for another missionary . . . to see to the buildings . . . so that I could be free to give the people the best medical care of which I was capable? . . .

---

[259] Ibid., pp. 40-41.

The following Wednesday evening, I mentioned all this to the church council and asked their prayer, that I might not become resentful. One godly man, after leading the group in believing prayer, smiled at me and offered a kindly rebuke.

"Doctor," he said, "when you are being a doctor, in your white coat, stethoscope round your neck, speaking French, you are miles from us. We fear you and all say: 'Yes, yes,' hardly even hearing what you said. But when you are down at the kiln with us, and your hands are rough as ours are: when you are out at the markets, using our language and making howlers and we all laugh at you: that's when we love you, and how we have come to trust you and can listen to what you tell us of God and His ways."[260]

Within a year the hospital building was completed. Now there was no more construction work demanding Helen's time and energy. This was what she had been waiting for, but perversely, she still wasn't satisfied.

My complaint was reversed. The hospital was built and functioning and the news had gone round. . . . And patients began streaming in. . . . I had not time for anything but medicine, medicine, medicine. . . . There was no let-up. . . . There was no off-duty. I had hoped to be a good missionary, to be able to . . . sit by bedsides . . . and tell the good news of salvation. But there was time for nothing but medicine. . . .

Again fortunately, I took my problem to the church elders for their prayers. Again they not only prayed for and comforted me, but also graciously rebuked me. "Doctor, how many patients come to this hospital daily?" . . .

"About two hundred to two hundred fifty." . . .

"Surely they come because you are here! They wouldn't come if there were no doctor. And what are we doing? . . . All day, every day, wherever you go, we go. . . . Doctor, do you realize we are having the joy. . . of leading five, ten, sometimes even more people to the Lord every week? If you weren't here they wouldn't come!" . . . .

---

[260] Ibid., pp. 71-72.

God had to teach me to be willing to be a member of a team.[261]

There were also lessons to be learned about prayer. Some lessons were about seemingly impossible prayers that were answered.

A woman died giving birth, leaving the premature newborn and a two-year-old daughter. There were no incubators because there was no electricity, so a hot water bottle was the way to keep a tiny baby warm enough during the drafty, cool nights. But in the humid tropics, rubber deteriorates rapidly. So when their last water bottle was filled for this baby, it burst. A nurse was assigned the sole task of holding that baby and keeping it warm with her own body heat.

The next day, Helen met with the orphanage children for their regular prayer time. She told them about the baby who needed to be kept warm and about the older sister, weeping because their mother was gone. Helen recorded the prayer of ten-year-old Ruth and her own response to that "impossible" prayer.

"Please, God . . . send us a hot water bottle. It'll be not good tomorrow, God, as the baby'll be dead, so please send it this afternoon. . . . And while You are about it, would You please send a dolly for the little girl, so she'll know You really love her?". . .

Could I honestly say, "Amen?" I just did not believe that God could do this. . . . The only way God *could* answer this particular prayer would be by sending me a parcel from the homeland. I had been in Africa almost four years at that time, and I had never, never received a parcel from home. . . .

By the time I reached home . . . there, on the veranda, was a large twenty-two pound parcel . . . bearing U.K. stamps. . . . I sent for the orphanage children. . . . Some thirty to forty pairs of eyes were focused on the large cardboard box.

[After pulling out several items], as I put my hand in again, I felt the . . . could it really be? I grasped it and pulled it out— yes, a brand new, rubber, hot water bottle! I cried. . . .

Ruth . . . rushed forward, crying out, "If God has sent the bottle, He must have sent the dolly too!" Rummaging down

---

[261] Ibid., pp. 72-74.

to the bottom of the box, she pulled out the small, beautifully dressed dolly. Her eyes shone! She had never doubted. . . .

That parcel had been on its way for five whole months . . . in answer to the believing prayer of a ten-year-old, to bring it "that afternoon."[262]

Some other lessons about prayer had to do with prayers that seemed not to be answered. At least, the answer was not the one that Helen wanted.

Helen had trained as a physician, but not as a surgeon. It was a frightening thing to think of learning to operate by doing it, when someone's life depended on her proficiency. She refused to operate until she was confronted with reality. Some people were going to die without surgery, and if she wouldn't do it, who could? For the rest of her time in Congo, she prayed for her fear to be lifted, but that was not the way God chose to keep her mind alert and hand steady.

## THAT I MAY KNOW HIM AND THE POWER OF HIS RESURRECTION

Helen continually dealt with the spiritual consequences of exhaustion and overwork. This apparently was another of the lessons for which God had brought her to Africa, so she would be within reach of the African colleagues God used to teach her. In at least two of her books she tells about one particular season of coming to the end of her rope and being hauled up by John Mangadima and Pastor Ndugu. This event happened about four years into her service in Congo.

Things had gone wrong at Nebobongo. I was very conscious that my life was not what it should have been. I was losing my temper with nurses, being impatient with the sick, getting irritated with workmen. . . . I was overwhelmingly tired, with an impossible work load and endless responsibilities.

The day came when on a medical ward-round in the hospital, I snapped at a woman patient. A small incident grew out of all proportion. . . . Everyone . . . listened in horrified amazement to the Christian missionary doctor, as she lost her temper in fluent Swahili.

We left the ward. . . . Very graciously and humbly, John Mangadima spoke to me. He had been my first student . . . and [was now] my first medical assistant.

"Doctor," he said, "I don't think the Lord Jesus would have spoken like that."

. . . How right he was . . . and yet where did I go next? I wanted to break down and cry, to run away, . . . but I could not. We went back to the Women's Ward, where I apologized. . . .

I struggled on through a few more frustratingly irritating weeks. I knew God was speaking to me, but I would not listen. . . . I piled up the excuses—my overweariness, my taut nerves, the load of responsibility. . . .

Then one morning at our Bible study hour, I broke down. The Holy Spirit was working in the hearts of African students and pupils and workmen, but not in my cold, hard heart, and I could bear no more.

Suddenly I knew that I had to get away from it all and sort myself out and seek God's forgiveness and restoration, if I was to continue in the work.

[Pastor Ndugu] had seen my spiritual need and made all the arrangements for me to go to stay in his village for a long weekend. . . . . There he gave me a room, and left me alone. I sought God's face for two unhappy days, but I could find no peace. . . . I knew I was quite unworthy of the title "missionary."

Sunday evening, Pastor Ndugu called me out to the fireside where he and his wife, Tamoma, were sitting. . . . We prayed. A great still silence wrapped us around. . . .

Gently he leaned toward me. "Helen . . . why can't you forget for a moment that you are white? You've helped so many Africans to find cleansing and filling and joy in the Holy Spirit through the blood of Jesus Christ. Why don't you let Him do for you what He has done for so many others?"

He . . . opened up to me hidden areas in my heart that I had hardly even suspected, particularly this one of race prejudice. I was horrified. . . . I was out there to share . . . the Good News of the gospel. I loved my African brethren. . . . But did I? The

Spirit forced me to acknowledge that subconsciously I did not really believe that an African could be as good a Christian as I was, or could know the Lord Jesus or understand the Bible as I did. My caring had in it an element of condescension, of superiority, of paternalism. . . . .

Opening his Bible at Galatians 2:20,[263] he drew a straight line in the dirt floor with his heel. "I," he said, "the capital I in our lives, Self, is the great enemy. . . .

"Helen . . . the trouble with you is that we can see so much Helen that we cannot see Jesus."

. . . My eyes filled with tears.

"I notice that you drink much coffee," he continued . . . apparently going off on a tangent. "When they bring a mug . . . to you . . . you stand there holding it, until it is cool enough to drink. May I suggest that every time, as you stand and wait, you should just lift your heart to God and pray . . ." and as he spoke, he moved his heel in the dirt across the I he had previously drawn, ". . . Please, God, cross out the I."

There in the dirt was his lesson of simplified theology— the Cross—the crossed-out I life. . . . "I have been crucified with Christ and I no longer live, but Christ lives in me" (Galatians 2:20).

I cycled back to Nebobongo. . . . Before I could say anything, John Mangadima burst out:

"Oh, Doctor, hallelujah! . . . You don't need to tell us, your face tells us. We've been praying for you for four years!"

And I had gone out to them as the missionary-teacher.[264]

God used illness to teach Helen even more deeply about humility and dependence. The doctor was not almighty. She too was often laid low.

During my years in Africa, I frequently became ill, often quite seriously so. During the first five years, besides recurrent bouts of . . . malaria, I had fairly severe amebic dysentery com-

---

[263] "I have been crucified with Christ. It is no longer I who live, but Christ who lives in me. And the life I now live in the flesh I live by faith in the Son of God, who loved me and gave himself for me."

[264] These quotes are woven together from the accounts in Living Holiness, pp. 67-68, and Living Sacrifice, pp. 45-48.

plicated by hepatitis. . . . Then, in 1957 . . . I was very ill indeed, with either meningitis or cerebral malaria. . . .

In my second term, I had a second bout of cerebral malaria and was ill for 3 months. . . . In my third term, I had tick-borne typhus fever and nervous exhaustion. . . .

Each time I was ill, another, African or missionary, who already had a full work load, had to give time to care for me. Someone else had to undertake my work in addition to his own. After each illness I became so depressed and discouraged, sensing that I was becoming a burden to the team and should go home. What was God trying to say to me? . . .

Why could God not keep me in good health? Of course, He could, but why did He not choose to do this? . . .

For years I was the only missionary doctor in our area, and so I was always needed. I was thus on the giving end, and the African was on the receiving end, always saying, "thank you." This . . . can soon become demoralizing. I had not seen that the roles needed to be reversed if the Africans were to know the same sense of fulfillment and joy in being needed that I knew.

Only when I was ill did I obviously, unequivocally need them. . . . They nursed me, they cared for me, they fed me, they washed me. And I said "Thank you"—and meant it.[265]

Helen's home in Congo could hardly have been a greater contrast to the places of service taken by her former fellow students from medical school. And yet for her it was home, perhaps all the more truly because of the depth of God's work in her there. She described Nebobongo as it was in 1962.

The scene is a small clearing in the north-eastern border of the mighty Ituri rain forest in Central Africa, just a couple of degrees north of the equator. . . . Rain, sunshine and a steamy humidity make up the climate: root vegetables and green leaves, soaked in palm oil, make up the diet. The normal additions of rice, peanuts and corn are sadly lacking as the rains came too late this year. . . . Shattering . . . poverty is the lot of everyone. . . . Suffering has abounded over centuries. Axe-wounds fester; colds develop into pneumonia; women die in childbirth; children die before they learn to walk. Yet the people are surprisingly happy, accepting with stoical resignation that life must include daily hardship.

Here in this small, almost unknown village, a hospital has grown up. . . . There is no electricity. Water is gathered in disused two-hundred-litre petrol drums, as it pours off the roofing during daily downpours. The medical staff seek to serve . . . half a million people . . . within a radius of 500 miles. . . . There is so little they can do with their extremely limited resources. . . . But they can and . . . do offer loving service with good nursing care.

A mile-long village borders the dirt-track road. . . . At the southern end of this village, two rows of small homes face each other across a sun-baked courtyard housing [the students] and the families of the fifteen workmen. Between the workmen's quarters and the hospital quadrangle lies the square of "rooms" where families and friends of hospital patients can stay, to cook the meals and wash the clothes and bandages of their sick relatives. The hospital itself consists of a motley collection of permanent brick and very impermanent mud wards, a room for surgical operations and a large, open, covered area for the outpatients' clinics.

The doctor's home, which backs on to the hospital compound, is the focal point of all the community's activities, looking out . . . on the village square, with its small church to the right and the primary school classrooms to the left. . . . Flanking all are . . . sloping grass lands, bright with frangipani and poinsettias, the whole surrounded by the eternal forest.

. . . Though to an outsider it may appear a little run-down and haphazard, to the team, whose very life blood has gone into its creation, it is a continuing source of wonder.

As for me, the doctor, Nebobongo is my life.[266]

Except for the addition of the hospital and paramedical training school, the town was as it had been for as long as anyone's great-great-

---

266 Roseveare, *Living Holiness*, pp. 11-13.

grandmother could remember. It might have been easy to assume that life would go on as it always had.[267]

## AND MAY SHARE IN HIS SUFFERINGS, BECOMING LIKE HIM IN HIS DEATH

But political currents were shifting and would sweep Nebobongo along in the undertow. On July 30, 1960, Belgium granted independence to the Belgian Congo. "Belgian" was dropped from the name, and the nation officially became Congo.

Just prior to this, reflecting the new spirit of nationalism, John Mangadima had become the first African appointed as Administrative Director of the medical center. Because Congo was now truly an African country, it became all the more important that the training school gain government accreditation.

Non-Africans in Congo felt unsettled in this time of changeover from Belgian to African authority. European governments removed their people from the country to protect them from possible backlash. But not all Europeans left. Helen remained.

> In July of 1960, three weeks after the declaration of Independence and twelve hours after the great evacuation of "white foreigners" from the north-eastern province, I was again sharply reminded of the reality of the love of God in the Christians around me. I was the only European left at our village of Nebobongo, and . . . National Army troops had driven through at dusk . . . threatening, with coarse laughter, to return during the night "to enjoy the white lady's company."
>
> . . . Fear had come into my home. I lay and tossed on my bed, allowing fear to . . . take possession of my reasoning faculties. A rat ran across the rafters and I shot upright, certain there was someone in the house. . . .
>
> . . . In desperation, I . . . got down on my knees, and simply asked God to hold me close to Himself. As . . . quietness

---

[267] After the uprising in the mid-1960s, life returned to its ages-long ways. A missionary visiting Ibambi in 2004 wrote about daily life in Ibambi, Helen's first home. This would be much the same as in Nebobongo, only a few miles away. "Teenage children have to fetch water from the stream and gather firewood everyday, as well as helping to grow food in their families' fields. They cook on an open stove made from three stones set on the ground. The evening meal, often the only meal of the day, can take at least four hours to prepare" (http://www.marpleparish.co.uk/Mission/sarah0104.htm, accessed 2/18/05).

regained possession of my vivid imagination, I asked . . . if it were possible, He would produce someone . . . to stay in my home with me. . . .

Bang! I nearly died! . . . "This is it! . . . They've come!" Again, a quiet knock . . . that sounded like a pistol shot. . . .

"Who's there?" I struggled to call out.

"It's only us!" whispered back two obviously female voices. . . . I opened the door in shattered relief, and welcomed Taadi, our evangelist's wife, and Damaris, our head midwife.

"Come in," I urged them, shutting the door quickly . . . behind them. . . . I sat down with my head in my hands, trying to recover . . . from the wave of shock . . . and then, dizzily, I asked why they had come.

"Well," said Taadi, "I woke from sleep and the Lord said to me very clearly, 'Go to the doctor, she needs you,' so I got up and came."

"That's exactly what happened to me!" exclaimed Damaris. . . .

We all three felt humbled and amazed at being part of the wonderful out-working of God's will.[268]

Four years after independence, there was a rebellion within the government. Guerrilla forces, calling themselves "Simbas," lions, tried to overthrow the Congolese government.

It was 1964. Rebel insurgents [the Simbas] had taken over the . . . province . . . driving out the National Army and imposing a fierce military regime over the terrified villagers. The occupying forces had a fierce bravado born of drugs, drink and witchcraft. They felt themselves to be invincible, and cruelly crushed any tiny spark of suspected resistance. . . .

One terrified student from our male nurses' school at Nebobongo came back to us from a weekend with his parents, . . . distraught. . . . Then he told us that "the streets were running with blood" and of . . . huge communal graves for upwards of five hundred. . . .

---

268 Roseveare, Living Holiness, pp. 84-86.

Revulsion and fear fought battles with my mind by day and in my dreams by night.

A pregnant woman was seized from our maternity complex, bound and thrown up on to a truck. As the soldiers drove off, we could not shut out her terrified screaming. . . .

Life became a living nightmare, but we had to go on living.

Whenever we could, we met together . . . to pray and read the Word of God and sing His praises, and so we kept sane, and God graciously replaced fear with peace.

After 10 dreadful weeks, the tide of war turned. The country's president . . . called in mercenary soldiers. . . . The army started to retake the country, repulsing the guerrillas, many of whom died in the new offensive.

"How can we die?" they asked themselves. Had they not been promised that, through the power of their initiation rites, no bullet could harm them? . . .

The only way the witch doctors could explain their loss of power was by the supposition of a stronger witchcraft in the hands of the advancing National Army. . . . This reversal had occurred with the arrival of white mercenary troops. It did not take much ingenuity to arrive at the conclusion that the white "doctors" had worked the needed [magic] to break the power of the guerrilla forces. So the rebels turned against every white doctor in their territory with frightening ferocity.[269]

Once again, when she was singled out for unwelcome and dangerous attention, God used his body—the body of Christ—to display to Helen his attentiveness. The medical center's truck had been hijacked by young guerrillas, and they forced Helen to drive it.

Amidst seventeen wild and armed youths, John and Joel climbed into the back of the truck in which I was being forced to drive these rebels to Wamba. . . . The vehicle had no lights, no self-starter, no windscreen wipers. Nervously fiddling with the pin of a hand grenade, the . . . teenage "lieutenant" of the gang had ordered me to drive into the courtyard of a . . . fac-

---

[269] Ibid., pp. 71-72.

tory, to search for petrol and oil. . . . Ordered out of the truck, I stood a few yards from it, alone in the dark.

That was when I first realized that John and Joel were with me. I sensed them . . . on either side of me. "Go away from me," I hissed to them. "They will kill me. Don't stand with me." . . .

"Doctor . . . that is why we are here. You shall not die alone!"

Half-an-hour later, when the rebels had driven off . . . leaving . . . us . . . alone in the rain, . . . Joel . . . said, "I felt like one of Daniel's three friends in the burning fiery furnace. Surely a fourth stood with us whose form was like that of the Son of God!" They had gone through that experience with me purely out of Christlike love. They did not need to be there![270]

One October night in 1964, her house was raided by Simbas, who destroyed and ransacked and plundered. When she tried to escape, she was battered, beaten, and her back teeth knocked out. With a gun pressed to her throbbing head, she prayed that God would just please let her die. When all the men except one had left, that one caught her, raped her, and arrested her.

She writes movingly of how abandoned she felt that night. "My God, my God, why have you forsaken me?" His answer to her was a removal of the fear as if it had been rinsed out of her—and a strong sense of his arms around her, holding her and comforting her. She felt as if he were saying, "When I called you to myself, I called you to the fellowship of my suffering (Philippians 3). They are not attacking you. They are attacking me. I'm just using your body to show myself to the people around you."

Over the next ten weeks, Helen was with various other people and held in several different places, including a convent. One young nun had been raped and felt as if she had betrayed God and her promises to God. Because of her similar experience, Helen was able to break through the woman's despairing barrier, as no one else could.

Just before her rescue, rebel soldiers were starting at one end of a large room, taking women away one by one and bringing them back after they were finished with them. Helen's first impulse was to hide and not have to bear this humiliation again. Then she thought of Jesus.

---

[270] Ibid., pp. 86-87.

He put himself forward as the substitute for us—*the fellowship of his suffering*. She moved to the front, to try to protect some of the other women from undergoing a new trauma they might possibly have escaped so far.

She looked back later on this whole period and wrote:

> We learned why God has given us His name as I AM (Exodus 3:14). His grace always proved itself sufficient in the moment of need, but never before the necessary time. . . . As I anticipated suffering in my imagination and thought of what these cruel soldiers would do next, I quivered with fear. . . . But when the moment came for action . . . he filled me with a peace and an assurance about what to say or do that amazed me and often defeated the immediate tactics of the enemy.[271]

Later, when she was back in England, a woman—a stranger—asked her if, in the midst of all the trouble, one particular October night had any significance. It was the very night of Helen's attack. The woman had been awakened with a strong sense to pray intensely for Helen, whom she only knew of. She prayed and didn't feel free to stop, until a certain time that she named to Helen. Given the difference in time zones, that was the same time that Helen had been washed through by the peace of God and had known that she wasn't abandoned by him.

## THAT BY ANY MEANS POSSIBLE I MAY ATTAIN THE RESURRECTION FROM THE DEAD

At the beginning of 1965, Helen and others were rescued by the National Army, and she returned to England. It was as if she had been raised from the dead. But she remembered her colleagues who did not live to return to their home countries. She thought of Hebrews 11, realizing that "by faith" she was taken out of Congo to return to her family; and equally "by faith" many friends were taken out of Congo to live immediately and forever with Christ.

After one year at home in England, she couldn't stay away. In 1966 she returned to a Congo (now renamed Zaire) struggling to recover from the Simba devastation. Five missions organizations were pooling

---

[271] Roseveare, *Living Sacrifice*, p. 95.

forces to create the Evangelical Medical Center of Nyankunde. Once again Helen was in the northeastern area of the country. Her charge was to establish the training and medical education aspect of the Center. After seven years, she returned to Britain to live. She writes:

> Since 1973, I have been living in the United Kingdom, and seeking to present the desperate need of the three thousand million people, alive today, who have never yet heard of our Lord Jesus Christ and of the redemption He wrought for them at Calvary. These are the "hidden peoples" in more than ten thousand ethnic groups around our world. As I try to present their needs, I pray earnestly that the Holy Spirit will stir hearts to make a response. It seems so obvious to me that Christian young people . . . should rise up and *go*. . . ."
>
> Why is the response so poor? . . .
>
> Is it that we Christians today have an inadequate under- standing of God's holiness and therefore of His wrath against sin and of the awfulness of a Christless eternity? If we were gripped by the two facts—of the necessity for judgment of sin because God is holy; and of the necessity of holiness in the Christian that he may represent such a God to others—would we not "hunger and thirst after righteousness" whatever the cost, and would not others then see Christ in us, and be drawn to Him?
>
> In other words, if we [understood] the Scriptural teaching on the need of Holiness in the life of every believer, we should not need to plead for missionaries.[272]

Helen Roseveare has returned more than once to her old African haunts. The video *Mama Luka Comes Home*[273] records her visit in the 1980s. Her former mission agency, WEC, reported her 2004 visit:

> The new operating theatre at Nebobongo was opened in mid- November with great joy and fanfare. It was named the 'Mama Luka Surgical Centre' in honour of Dr. Helen Roseveare (UK) [who did her first Caesarian here some 50 years ago.]. . .

---

[272] Roseveare, *Living Holiness*, p. 32.
[273] Vision Video, 1992.

The Tuesday following the opening, Philip Wood and the young Nebobongo doctors inaugurated the new operating room by doing surgery on a nine month old baby with a harelip. The child is the grandson of Joshua who has worked for many years in the print shop at Ibambi. The operation went off smoothly and the report the next morning was that the baby was feeding well.[274]

The work continues at Ibambi and Nebobongo. Today, Helen Roseveare lives in Britain, still writing and witnessing.[275] In 1987, she remembered an encounter with an African herdsman who could not read and another with a British woman.

One morning in 1972, just before I left the mission field, I had the shattering privilege of meeting an African at a roadside in Uganda. After the customary greetings and courtesies, as he stood and looked at me, I asked him what he wanted. He said to me in Swahili, "Are you a sent one?"

Startled by his question, I thought quickly that this is what the word missionary means, and I said to him, "Yes, I am, but it depends, sent by whom for what?" And he said to me, "Are you a sent one by a great God to tell me about something called Jesus?"

I confess I gasped. "Can you read?" I asked him.

"No," he answered. . . .

I took . . . a five-colored wordless book that we use to help those who cannot read understand the way of salvation. And in the early-morning sunshine I sat beside him and had the unique joy of leading him to the Lord Jesus Christ. . . .

A few years ago [in Britain] . . . as I stood on the railroad platform with my umbrella up, a woman . . . did not have an umbrella, so I offered to share mine. . . . I thought quickly, "How can I start a conversation with her?"

On the other side of the railway tracks was a large adver-

---

274 WEC, January 2005, Online Newsletter, http://www.wec-usa.org/prayer/africa.html.

275 Other books by Helen Roseveare not mentioned in these notes are: *Living Fellowship* (London: Hodder and Stoughton, 1992); *Doctor Among Congo Rebels* (London: Lutterworth Press, 1965); *Doctor Returns to Congo* (London: Lutterworth Press, 1967). Her books are not easy to find. Some are available from her former mission agency: WEC International, P.O. Box 1707, 709 Pennsylvania Ave., Ft. Washington, PA 19034-8707, 888-646-6202; http://www.wec-int.org/.

tisement for cigarettes. I said to her, "That makes me angry. . . . That poster makes young people want to smoke. Smoking causes lung cancer. Lung cancer causes death." And right there on the railway platform she broke down and cried.

The train came in . . . and sitting beside her, I asked if I could help. She said, "I've just come from the city hospital . . . and they told me I am dying of lung cancer because I have smoked all my life." As I realized God's overruling of our conversation, I heard her add, "And I don't know where I'm going." . . .

I took out . . . a little tiny copy of that same five-colored wordless book. True, I blushed from ear to ear because the whole compartment listened in while I shared with her . . . the exact same way of salvation that I had taught an illiterate herdsman on an African roadside. There was no difference.

It doesn't matter whether I travel 6,000 miles or just twenty minutes from home. . . . What matters is whether the people we meet matter to us as much as they matter to God.[276]

The outward circumstances of Helen Roseveare's life may be different from that of many of us, but her inner battles were the same. And as we all know, our inner battles don't stay inside. They spill out and injure innocent bystanders, usually the people that we care about the most.

Seeing the battles in someone else's life—Helen Roseveare's, in this case—can give us perspective to understand more clearly our own struggles. One thing I have seen here is that there is seldom just one cause for our valleys. We see how tangled the causes are of spiritual dryness as Helen describes a period during her medical training.

The joy and excitement of the first three years suddenly seemed to drain away. . . . Work began to get on top of me; unhappiness, loneliness, fear, inferiority, all began to be acutely present. At the same time Bible study and prayer became perfunctory instead of joyous. . . . Witness continued, but with no real faith or expectation of seeing results. Looking back it is easy to real-

276 http://www.urbana.org/_articles.cfm?RecordId=534 (accessed 2/18/05).

ize that at least part of the explanation lies in the fact that, like many of my fellow medical students, I was suffering from over-work and strain resulting from a very full programme. . . . I . . . thought this exhaustion meant spiritual failure.[277]

She felt like a spiritual failure. And in some sense she was. She dragged herself to her Bible reading and prayer. There seemed to be no point in talking about Christ. She probably felt like a hypocrite when she did, because who would want the kind of spiritual life she had? And yet, that deadness didn't come from nowhere. She was working and studying too many hours in a day, which meant she wasn't getting enough sleep. Her vulnerability to "unhappiness, loneliness, fear, infe-riority" came from two directions: from her exhaustion and from her lack of spiritual energy. Her spiritual life dragged because she was exhausted, and she was exhausted because of her low spiritual life. In other words, it was all one tangle.

That is a good lesson for us to remember. Inasmuch as we have a choice, we need to make good choices about sleeping and eating and other things that affect our health, so that we don't open ourselves to sin that undermines our spiritual well-being.

And from the other side, we need to work hard to keep our con-nection with God strong, through his Word and our prayer, so that we have the perception to see when we are sliding into bad attitudes and the likelihood of glossing over and justifying sin in our lives.

God often uses other people to drag us back when we've slidden into the sins that flourish in spiritual dryness. We see this happen in Helen's life. It's a humbling thing to have other people point out our weaknesses, our *sins*. My inclination is to justify myself, thinking they just don't know all the factors that made me do or speak as I did.

I was especially encouraged to see Helen turning to her African pastor and co-workers and receiving exhortation and correction from them. Even when we don't want to be racist or prejudiced, and though we wouldn't admit it to ourselves, it's hard to believe that someone from another culture can understand or even have the right to admonish us. That's especially true when, as Helen exclaimed, "And I had gone out to them as the missionary-teacher!"[278]

---

[277] Roseveare, *Give Me This Mountain*, pp. 56-57.
[278] Roseveare, *Living Sacrifice*, p. 48.

It is a blessed gift when God gives us hearts and minds to know, to feel, to realize that brothers and sisters come in every color, that "in Christ Jesus [we] are all sons of God, through faith. For as many of [us] as were baptized into Christ have put on Christ. There is neither Jew nor Greek, there is neither slave nor free, there is neither male nor female, for [we] are all one in Christ Jesus" (Galatians 3:26-28).

I learned something else from Helen Roseveare. Maybe it wasn't *learning*; maybe it was reminding me what I should already know. When things were falling apart at Nebobongo, and Helen knew she needed a change, how did she express it? She said, "Suddenly I knew that I had to get away from it all *and sort myself out and seek God's forgiveness and restoration*, if I was to continue in the work."[279] When things are bad, we try to take a break and relax. But is that all we do? Really, taking a break will do little good unless it not only takes us away from the mess but also turns us toward God.

Perhaps the deepest underlying personal factor in Helen's tension was the need she felt to do her very best and, if possible, to be the very best. God called her to Africa where that was not possible. There were continuing lessons for her: learning to treat malaria by symptoms rather than with prescribed lab tests, having to operate without having been trained as a surgeon, needing to make bricks rather than spending the day with patients.

Perhaps that is an issue for some of us—struggling with the reality that God has called us to do less than we want to do or less than what we believe is best. That can happen in any setting. For me, it's been especially true in my years with small children—"I got a college degree for *this*?" Maybe our problem is the way we see ourselves. Maybe we think more highly of ourselves than we ought.

If anyone was too good to die, it was Jesus. If anyone should have done greater things than walking dusty roads and talking with people too dense to understand him, it was Jesus. In Philippians 3, the passage that headlines Helen's story, is the verse, "that I may know him and the power of his resurrection, and may share his sufferings, becoming like him in his death" (verse 10). When God called Helen to less than she expected, he was helping her become like Christ, rather than like the best doctor or missionary she knew of. Who is it that we want to be like?

---

[279] Roseveare, *Living Holiness*, p. 67 (emphasis added).

In 1989, 120 young people sat cross-legged in the Piper living room and dining room, covering nearly every square inch of floor space. They had accepted our open invitation to anyone who thought missions might be in his or her future.

As Helen Roseveare stood by our fireplace and looked into their faces, she reached backward toward the mantel and eased a long-stemmed red rosebud from a tall vase. As she spoke, she broke off the thorns, the leaves, the petals, the green outer layer of stem—every element that makes a rose a rose. All that was left was a lithe, straight shaft. The pieces that lay on the floor were not bad things. But, she explained, they had to be removed if she were going to make an arrow. God does this to us, she said. He removes everything—even innocent, good things—that hinders us from being the arrows that he will shoot for his purposes at his intended target.

*I have been moved by parallels between the lives of Helen Roseveare and one of my sisters. Julie's call to Africa began with a college mission trip more than thirty years ago. Home has been in Central African Republic, Kenya, Cameroon, Congo Brazzaville, and Cameroon again. She has lived through four coups and attempted coups, been evacuated twice with her family, and has dealt with the internalized stress that remained afterward. Still she has returned each time because she can't stay away. And so this story of Helen Roseveare in Congo Kinshasa is dedicated to Julie Anderson, in Cameroon with Steve and their son, Luke.*

*Julie, I listen gratefully as you sing[280] the "crossed-out I" words that I believe could also be Helen Roseveare's.*

> *Not I, but Christ, be honored, loved, exalted,*
> *Not I, but Christ, be seen, be known, be heard,*
> *Not I, but Christ, in every look and action,*
> *Not I, but Christ, in every thought and word.*
>
> *Not I, but Christ, to gently soothe in sorrow,*
> *Not I, but Christ, to wipe the falling tear,*

---

[280] Julie Anderson, *In His Grip*, privately produced CD (2002), julie_anderson@sil.org.

*Not I, but Christ, to lift the weary burden,*
*Not I, but Christ, to hush away all fear.*

*Not I, but Christ, no idle word e'er falling,*
*Christ, only Christ, no needless bustling sound,*
*Christ, only Christ, no self-important bearing,*
*Christ, only Christ, no trace of I be found.*

*Not I, but Christ, my every need supplying,*
*Not I, but Christ, my strength and health to be;*
*Christ, only Christ, for body, soul, and spirit,*
*Christ, only Christ, live then Thy life in me.*

*Christ, only Christ, e're long will fill my vision;*
*Glory excelling soon, full soon I'll see*
*Christ, only Christ, my every wish fulfilling—*
*Christ, only Christ, my all in all to be.*[281]

---

[281] A. B. Simpson, "Christ, Only Christ."

# Resources from Noël Piper

### Treasuring God in Our Traditions
*Crossway Books, 2003*

Traditions can be ordinary, everyday habits, or they can be "especially" traditions for holidays such as Christmas or Easter. Every God-centered tradition can be an adhesive that holds a family together and an anchor in the harbor of the family, reflecting our true refuge in God.

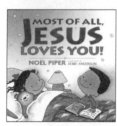

### Most of All, Jesus Loves You
*Crossway Books, 2004*

A loving bedtime ritual reminds a pre-schooler of the great truth that of all the people who love him or her, Jesus loves the most!

This tract —
available in English or Spanish —
is adapted from the book of the same title.

### Noël Calendar
*A Family Tradition for the Generations*

Noël's Advent calendar helps families focus on their true treasure. It's an excellent gift for weddings, new babies, and Christmas.

## ✳ desiringGod

Desiring God is a ministry that exists to spread a passion for the supremacy of God in all things for the joy of all peoples through Jesus Christ. We love to spread the truth that God is most glorified in us when we are most satisfied in him.

We invite you to visit desiringGod.org, where you'll find free sermon manuscripts, articles and audio downloads. Our online store allows you to purchase audio albums, God-centered children's curricula, and books and resources by John Piper or Noël Piper. You can find information about our radio ministry at desiringGodradio.org.

DG also has a whatever-you-can-afford policy, designed for individuals without discretionary funds. If you'd like more information about this policy, please contact us at the address or phone number below.

We exist to help you treasure Jesus Christ above all things. If we can serve you in any way, please let us know!

---

**Desiring God**
2601 East Franklin Avenue
Minneapolis, MN 55406-1103

Telephone: 1.888.346.4700
Fax: 612.338.4372
Email: mail@desiringGod.org
Web: www.desiringGod.org